How to become a
RECORD
PRODUCER

David Mellor

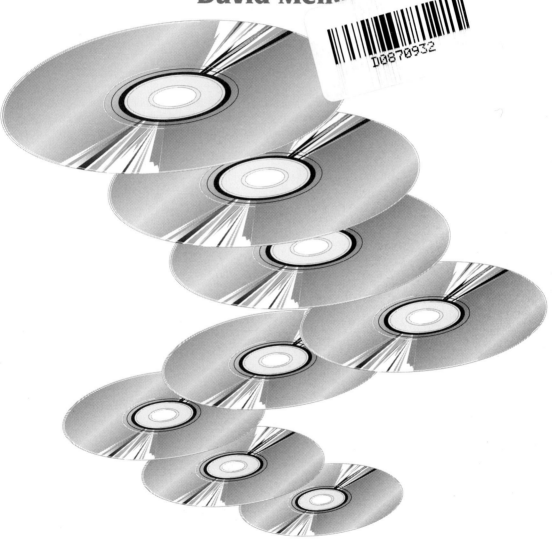

PC Publishing

PC Publishing
Export House
130 Vale Road
Kent TN9 1SP
UK

Tel 01732 770893
Fax 01732 770268
email pcp@cix.compulink.co.uk
web site http://www.pc-pubs.demon.co.uk

First published 1998

ISBN 1 870775 48 1

British Library Cataloguing in Publication Data
A catalogue record for this book is available from the British Library

Printed in Great Britain by Bell and Bain, Glasgow

Introduction

You love music. No, wait a minute, you really *love* music. Music is your whole life and you think about little else. But you don't just love listening to music, or wearing the hair style or T-shirt of your favourite act, you want to create music and give to others what gives you most pleasure yourself. You could consider becoming a singer or songwriter, or a musician, but you realise that to become an artist in your own right you have to become involved with a lot of things that are not music – creating an image, photo sessions, promotion, interviews. And to become a musician is only ever to take part in the creation and performance of music – but taking part just isn't enough.

If this description fits you, then there is only one possible choice for your career in life – to become a record producer. To be a record producer is to be the one person who moulds, shapes, masterminds and oversees the creation of music from raw chords and lyrics, through performance and creation in the studio, to a finished album ready for the world to hear and enjoy. The record producer is the ultimate musician and the recording studio is his or her instrument. The world's biggest, most complex and most expensive instrument in fact – and the most difficult to master.

Fortunately, it's easy to set out on the path towards being a record producer. All you need are a couple of musicians to work with, and a friend with a simple four track recorder. Make a recording, then figure out how you can make it better. If you have the ears, you will hear something new every time you record, and each experience will bring you one step closer to being able to get people to pay you for doing what you enjoy most. Be warned however, that it is a steep path to success, and you will need every ounce of determination you can muster.

Only hard work and experience in real studio situations can teach you how to make a record, any producer will tell you that - and they will also tell you how they got into production because they had the talent and they got lucky. This book explains how producers work and who they work with, and also tells you the best ways to get into the business. So there's no need to record purely for your own amusement and only dream about doing it for a living. Fire up your enthusiasm and determination and read on, and you will learn *How to Become a Record Producer*.

Contents

1 What is a record producer?

*I*n the course of my work I meet literally hundreds of young people who want to get involved with music, recording and sound engineering in one way or another. When asked what their ultimate ambition might be, 'To be a record producer' is probably the most common answer. But out of every 100 people who want to become record producers, perhaps only one has the raw talent. Out of a 100 people with the raw talent only one will have the determination. And out of a 100 people with the raw talent and determination, only one will ever get the opportunity!

This is how difficult it is to become a record producer, and I could go on to say that only a small proportion of people who ever get a production credit go on to develop a serious and lasting career in the business. But if it is so difficult to become a record producer, why do so many find it so attractive? I have to say that the vast majority of people that I meet who want to become producers don't seem to have much idea of what the job entails. They are attracted by the 'glamour' of the record industry, by the possibility of socialising with the stars, and by the prospect of a fat pay cheque at the end of each successful project – the three myths of record production one might say.

To take care of each of these myths in turn: The glamour in the music industry is created by a massive publicity machine for the benefit of the public at large. For the people working in the industry it is a job of work. An immensely satisfying and enjoyable job perhaps, but certainly not glamorous.

The idea of mixing with the stars may be attractive initially, but once you have met a few you begin to realise that they are mostly pretty ordinary people. They may happen to have an extraordinary talent in one way or another but the majority are still normal human beings in every other sense. You will enjoy being able to tell people at parties who you have met or worked with recently and bask in a little reflected glory, but to you these people – apart from their talent of course – won't be anything out of the ordinary.

There are certainly a number of people who make a lot of money but most people working in music probably don't make as much as they could out of an 'ordinary' job. For instance, even if you were among the top 10% of songwriters and composers, you might still not earn enough money to call it your living.

By now I'm sure I have put off anyone who is attracted to record production for the wrong reasons, and I can take it that those of you who are still reading are serious about becoming producers. But exactly what is a record producer? What do they actually do to earn their living and status?

I think the best way is to look back in history to a stage where a recording was seen as a live performance captured on vinyl, rather than the studio constructions that are now the norm. In those days it was pretty much taken for granted that an act that was worth recording could perform, and nothing more than the performance was needed for the record. All that was necessary was a studio, and perhaps a little musical help in the form of an arranger, musical director and session musicians. The project was overseen by the A&R (which stands for Artists and Repertoire, or Artists and Recording in some companies) department of the record company to make sure

Beatles producer George Martin at Air Lyndhurst London

that everything was progressing as it should. Effectively, the A&R manager was the producer, and to a certain extent modern A&R departments still have a significant influence on how a record is produced.

Gradually, the process of recording became more of an act of creation in its own right, rather than the replication of a live performance. A distinct role of producer was created, and gradually, following the lead of The Beatles' producer George Martin, they split from the record companies and became freelance workers or set up their own production companies.

Although there is no strict definition of the term 'record producer', I think it is worth emphasising that in this book I will be thinking of the record (or CD or cassette) as the end product. There are people who can be called 'recording producers' who do the same job but the product goes elsewhere, into broadcasting or film perhaps. No disrespect to recording producers of course, your job is just as demanding, but not as glamorous!

Within record production I have discovered a number of distinct styles of work and I think it is worth covering each of these in outline so that readers with talent and ambition can start deciding where their future may lie. In the coming chapters I will describe, with the help of top record producers, the production process from initial concept to final pay cheque.

Hopefully, by the end of the book you will know exactly what steps you have to take to become a record producer and, given the right opportunities, you will be able to take your talent as far as it will go.

Engineer producer

One of the other great myths about record production, beside the three I mentioned earlier, is that you need to be first and foremost a genius with studio equipment. This is absolutely not true, because the equipment is only a means to an end. Many engineers have just a basic technical knowledge and would privately admit that they are far from knowing every last detail about every piece of equipment in the studio.

> One of the myths of record production is that you need to be first and foremost a genius with studio equipment.

One has to remember too that equipment is designed by electronic and software engineers, not music recording engineers, and although most manufacturers do their utmost to ensure that their products are exactly what recording engineers need (even if recording engineers themselves don't always know how they would like technology to progress!), inevitably most modern pieces of equipment offer a range of functions far in excess of real life practicality. 80% of engineering is not technical knowledge, it is knowing when something sounds right. And what's more, knowing what to do to make something that sounds almost right, exactly right in its musical context.

3

So if you know how to route signals around a mixing console, and you know how to operate the basic outboard equipment, then the rest of it is really down to listening. Your ears will tell you which microphones to use and where to place them, they will also tell you when to use EQ and compression, and what settings to use. And as you develop your experience they will also tell you when a musical idea is working and when it isn't.

This last point is where the boundary between engineering and production lies, and I believe that you don't need to be a musician of any kind to develop from an engineer into a producer along this route. Any engineer will start by learning the basic equipment operation, and how to spot technical faults in a recording like excessive noise, clicks or distortion. But once a reasonable degree of technical mastery is achieved, then I don't think it is unreasonable to say that you have achieved a musical status equivalent to an arranger or musical director. You may not be able to bash out a tune on an instrument, but an arranger won't be able to say that if a guitar line isn't working in the studio, all it needs is a bit of compression and chorus (for example) and a slightly different playing technique, and then it will work.

The engineer producer who lacks conventional musical skills will probably work with a band that can supply all the necessary musical knowledge, and translate their work from a brilliant stage performance into an equally effective studio recording.

Musician producer

A musician producer might be strongly tempted to influence the music rather than the sound of the band. But of course, many bands are receptive to new musical ideas and want to acquire outside influences to ensure that each new CD is a musical step forward rather than more of the same. I think you will know of bands in both categories!

Although many producers have come up through the engineering route, you don't need any technical knowledge at all to produce, as long as you can communicate effectively with someone who does know the equipment. I think this point is more easily understood if you think of the director of a TV commercial. The director will be very visually aware, and will know what can be achieved with telecine and digital video effects. He or she cannot be expected to be a technical expert, but as long as there is good communication between the director and the telecine operator and digital artists, then the result can be visually amazing.

So the musician producer needs to know what can be achieved in the studio, but someone else will be pushing the faders. A musician is obviously in a much better position than an engineer to know how to put together a piece of music for a recording from scratch, and a musician producer will often be an arranger as well, putting together all the musical lines and colours, whether natural or synthesised,

4

that will make up the finished track. A musician producer could take on a solo singer much more easily than an engineer producer could, and he or she could obviously also produce a band. It really depends on attitude, and the one thing that successful producers have in common is that they have a clear image in their mind of the importance of the final product. Anything that helps the final product is good and worth doing, anything that doesn't contribute to the product is a waste of time.

It would be a waste of time trying to impose ideas onto a band that already knew their way round the studio and had a clear idea of what they wanted to sound like, and also had a proven track record of being able to satisfy their market.

Executive producer

As well as the engineer producer and musician producer there is a third type which I shall call the 'executive producer'. The executive producer doesn't know anything about engineering nor about music. 'So how do they produce?', you ask. The answer is that they know all the people they need with the technical and musical skills to handle all the elements of production, and most importantly, they know when something sounds right. They don't need to be present all the time in the studio, they just need to hear work in progress occasionally. Their instinct will tell them whether the product is marketable or not. Nice work if you can get it, you may say, and I suppose it must be.

DJs often find their way into production along this route, because they are in a better position than anyone else in the industry to know what will and what will not please an audience. The difference between something that sells and something that ends up on a cut price market stall may be incredibly small, but at least in dance music, the DJ will be able to recognise that difference.

Freelance producer

Any type of producer may work as a freelance producer. In this situation a record company might have signed a band or act and be scouting round for someone to put it all together in the studio. Obviously all the producers know the record company A&R people, and the A&R people know who the key producers are. Matching an act with a producer is an important A&R skill.

Sometimes the decision will be made on a 'flavour of the month' basis. If a producer has had a series of successful records, then he

The producer's view – Stephen Street

Stephen Street is a producer with both a musical and an engineering background. Bands he has produced include The Smiths, Blur and The Cranberries.

Musical versus engineering skills

'I would say that to be a producer you have to be 80 to 90 percent a musician. There are people who are especially good at knowing how to balance sound and I suppose their career really should be more in mixing rather than production.'

On the SSL mixing console

'I reckon I only use about 60 to 70 percent of what it's capable of, but that's enough for me. Ergonomically, I think the SSL is a very well laid out piece of equipment and I think the computer is very easy to use. I have learned it well enough to know how to do what I want to do.'

Getting work

'Normally acts come to me but the one exception was Blur. I heard their first single and said to their manager, 'I love that band and I would like to work with them if they are looking for anyone'. They were going to carry on using the same guy they had used for their first single but in their next session it didn't quite work out. So I got a call saying would I like to have a go? I went in with them and it was a success straight away, and I have been with them for four albums now.'

Oddly enough, Stephen Street's first production credit was for the same artist (Karl Blake in Shock Headed Peters' I Bloodbrother Be) for whom the author of this book received his first engineering credit (Karl Blake a few years earlier in The Lemon Kittens' We Buy a Hammer for Daddy).

may be seen as being on a roll and the next production will be a big seller too. But the act and the producer must also be compatible in some way. Perhaps they will share the same musical vision, and have a deep understanding of the style of music in which they work. Perhaps they will also get along well together because they are musically in tune. On the other hand, perhaps a band is wilful and potentially difficult to work with. The producer must be capable of exercising a degree of control to shape the band into something that will work on CD as well as it does on stage. Maybe an older and more experienced producer will have more respect in the band's eyes, or maybe they need someone who is able to share their vision and

The producer's view – Mike Pickering and Paul Heard of M People

M People don't use a producer. Co-writers Mike Pickering (the band's founder) and Paul Heard produce themselves, starting in their home studio working out ideas and laying down basic tracks, and moving to a top commercial studio such as The Strongroom in London for recording.

How they became involved in production

Paul Heard: 'I was the bass player in Orange Juice  (with Edwyn Collins) for about two years and I was working more and more in the studio with Edwyn. Because I was comfortable in the studio and I had some good ideas I started becoming more involved in production.'

Mike Pickering: 'I got involved when I was with Factory Records and I was in a band and we couldn't afford producers. The first real production I did myself was for the Happy Mondays. It's a process of finding out and learning in the studio.'

M People

Mike Pickering: 'M People was my project initially. I was doing so many productions and remixes and I wanted to be more on the creative side. I wanted to do an album of songs with people I liked. Heather (Heather Small, M People's vocalist) was one of the people I wanted to work with and it just clicked.'

Paul Heard: 'M People is completely self contained, we write and produce everything ourselves. We have never worked with a different producer. The last ten years have been a learning process. The more you are in the studio, the more you learn.'

Recording technology

Paul Heard: 'We have been recording for a number of years and we have built up a team where everyone is comfortable with their roles. We have an engineer, and a programmer as well, whom we often use. They know our sound exactly, what kind of equalisation and what kind of compression. They work towards the sound they know we want to hear. It's important to know what the technology can do, but I'm not that interested in being 'hands on'.'

Mike Pickering: 'I understand what the equipment can achieve, but it doesn't really suit me and I don't really bother with it. I prefer to work with Paul, standing by the piano with a dictaphone or small tape recorder on top. He'll play chords and I'll sing what I think. If you are using computers you tend to start with the track, but we like to concentrate on the melody. We use a programmer for sounds. We ask him for a certain sound and then leave him to it for half an hour. If you spend all your time looking at a screen it dulls your creativity.'

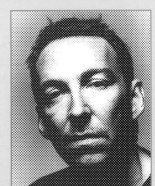

Mike Pickering

will simply smooth over whatever rough edges need to be smoothed (and leave well alone the rough edges that need to remain rough!).

The freelance producer will be paid by the record company (who will get that money back from the band's share of the eventual profits) and he or she is then free to go on to work for another record company as they please.

M People – Paul Heard, Shovel,
Heather Small and Mike Pickering

Entrepreneur producer

'Entrepreneur producer' is a title I have invented to cover the type of
producer who initiates a project and then sells it to a record company
in the form of an act with writing, recording and management
already in place, or as a partly developed idea working towards the
same end.

Either way, the producer or producers will be at the top of the
food chain and will receive the lion's share of the rewards. The
project could be a band in which the producer takes the roles of
songwriter and musician, with a front man or woman to handle the
vocals and provide a focus for the marketing machine to work on.

Alternatively, the producer might be an engineer or musician who
takes on the role of A&R scout and looks for a band or singer to
work with. There will probably be a certain amount of investment
involved since the band will need studio time and promotional
material will need to be prepared.

The entrepreneur producer will need to be able to promise the
band or singer the earth, and give the impression that he is capable
of delivering it. A track record of success will of course help!

One of the advantages of working in this way is in the payoff. Not
only will the entrepreneur producer be entitled to a larger slice of the

financial cake, he or she is also in control of an ongoing project which will hopefully continue to be successful, rather than staggering from each one-off project to the next.

2 Pre-production

*T*he natural habitat of the record producer is often assumed to be the recording studio, for obvious reasons. But only part of the process of making a successful recording takes place there, the final part. Before the producer and band or artist enter the studio there is likely to be a period of pre-production to work on the music and the arrangements, to allow the musicians and producer to develop their ideas. To do all of this in a studio costing several hundreds of pounds a day would be wasteful. Of course, there are some bands who practically live in the studio from day one.

If you can afford it, this way of working has a lot to commend it since it not only concentrates the effort, it allows spontaneity and encourages experimentation. If the tape is rolling continually, there is every opportunity for the magic of the moment to be captured for further development. But as I said, only a few top selling bands and artists could afford to work in this way in a commercial studio.

The Rolling Stones have been widely reported as coming into the studio with their instruments, entourage and hardly anything else – certainly no musical ideas.

Assessing the demo

Suppose you specialise in producing bands. Your first point of contact with the band will be either a live performance or a demo tape. This would apply whether you were initiating the project yourself or if you had been engaged by a record company. A live performance many not tell you much apart from whether the band has the ability to generate excitement and interest in the audience, but it may tell you where the balance lies between the appeal of the band's members as musicians or personalities and the appeal of the music itself. As far as selling product goes, it has to be said that sometimes the music is simply a means to an end. If the band do have the ability to excite the audience, and excite you as a producer of course, then a demo tape will allow more critical assessment of the material. It will be your job to supervise the transformation of these rough and ready home recordings into a professional product, and this transformation is definitely not going to happen all by itself.

People in the music industry generally fall into three types: those who don't know if they like something unless they can see that someone else likes it; those who can see talent when it is shoved in their face; and finally those very few people who can see *potential.* A producer must be able to recognise the presence or absence of potential in a band or a song from a very rough recording.

Although high quality recording equipment is available at a low enough cost for almost everyone to afford, it doesn't turn people into producers overnight, and the demo tape of what may turn out to be a totally brilliant song may disguise the worth of that song almost to the point of invisibility. Conversely, many demos have been sent out that are very well recorded from a technical point of view, but the spark of excitement and originality is sadly lacking.

Developing the song

Once the producer has spotted the potential in a song, then his or her next job would be to think of ways in which this potential could be brought out to best advantage. A musically orientated producer (as opposed to engineering orientated) may start thinking about the arrangement and structure of the song and may virtually rearrange the whole thing before even going through the studio door. Or he may just allow ideas to develop at their own pace, knowing that the band will probably be able to take on these ideas and develop them still further. Also at this stage, the producer will be thinking of what the potential problem areas might be. Is the drummer any good, for example, and can the singer sing in tune?

Still at the demo stage, the producer may also play a part in selecting which songs go on the album (the record company will decide which songs are released as singles). With a band, the producer may simply hint very strongly that a certain song is not really up to it, and that they should write a few more that are similar to one he prefers. With a solo artist who is not a songwriter, the producer may have such a degree of control that he is choosing all of the songs and merely acknowledging the singer's preferences. The role of song selection might be extended and the producer may say that he likes a song, but it needs certain changes.

For example, if a song has the potential to be a single, then whatever it has that gives it that potential must happen very early on or it won't stand a cat in hell's chance of getting radio plays. If the producer is a songwriter himself, then he may add ideas to the song, or even partially rewrite the song. In extreme cases the producer may end up getting a co-writer credit and a share of the ensuing royalties.

If the drummer is at the 'good for an amateur' stage, then options might include lots of rehearsal, a few lessons with a pro, acceptance that the band is what it is, or directing the person in question politely to the 'Musicians Available' columns in the music weeklies. No-one said that being a producer was going to be easy and whatever it takes to get a good recording, that's what the producer has to do.

Rehearsal

Rehearsal can take place in any or all of three locations: at the producer's or artist's home, at a rehearsal studio, at the recording studio. These are listed in order of rising cost. For some styles of recording, particularly using experienced session musicians (who may charge rates well in excess of the Musicians' Union minimum) it may be cost-effective to rehearse during the session, just prior to the recording. But for a band, the members all have a financial interest in the success of their recording so their rehearsal time comes free and doesn't impose any additional loading on the budget.

Home studio

Early rehearsals are conveniently done at home. Song structure is easily plotted with just voice and guitar or keyboard. This would be a good time to alter lyrics or to tinker with the melody line of the song. Most singers have a fairly narrow range of notes over which their voice is at its best, so the key of the song can be changed either upwards so the vocalist can project more effectively, or downwards so that the highest notes can be reached comfortably. There is always the option at this point to choose a key that is slightly uncomfortably high, because the singer doesn't have to do the song all in one go and can do as many takes and punch ins as necessary.

Choosing a key that is slightly high does of course store up a problem for later live performances, but the producer will be off working on another project by this time!

Rehearsal studio

A rehearsal studio is good place to work on arrangements, and to allow the members of the band to settle into their performances. Once upon a time it was normal for a band to write some songs, go off on tour with them, and then record the album. Now of course, a band goes on tour to promote their new CD.

There is a balance to be struck between the amount of rehearsal necessary for the band to perform to the best of their ability and the risk of over-rehearsing, which is not to be underestimated. Sometimes the right amount of rehearsal will be practically none at all and the first time that the band plays the song all the way through without making a mistake will be their best performance ever. That obviously should be the one that is recorded.

Although excessive rehearsing can detract from spontaneity, it gives the opportunity to try out different arrangements. Perhaps the first rhythm that the drummer and bass player settle into isn't the best one for the song. Perhaps experimenting with another way of playing the song will give a fresh insight on the original and make the performance better.

There is occasionally one final – very final – stage of rehearsal. This is where the band goes into the studio with the producer and records a couple of songs. The A&R manager listens to the recordings, decides they are no good and fires the producer!

Budget recording studio

Although the rehearsal studio is obviously a good place to rehearse, an even better place may be a budget recording studio, depending on the band and on how the producer wants to work. Now there is the risk that something may be recorded, just as a tryout, but the recording isn't technically up to full professional standard and the same 'vibe' proves impossible to recapture. Everyone who is involved in recording will experience this sooner or later.

Programming

In the parallel universe of sequenced music then the rehearsal stage takes quite a different form. It isn't sensible at the highest professional level to record a band in anything other than a proper studio, but it is perfectly viable to sequence tracks at home and then take all your MIDI and computer equipment into the studio and transfer your work onto tape.

Emu Orbit, Carnaval and Planet Phatt – an exciting trio of sound modules

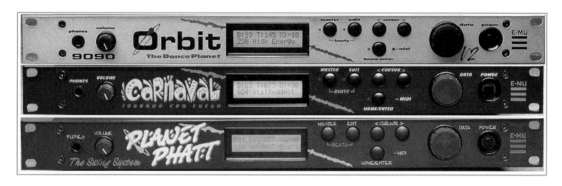

Although there is something to be said for experiencing great sound on big studio monitors while you are programming, it isn't really cost effective to do this when you can work for free with no time pressure in the privacy of your own home studio. In sequenced music it is far more common for the writer/musician to be his or her own engineer and producer all at the same time, at least at the programming stage, and then continue to produce in a commercial studio while a specialist engineer handles the faders. In band recording there is always the difficulty of recognising when something is 'good enough', which is an important part of the producer's skill. In sequenced recording, 'perfection' is easily attainable and the producer's skill is more biased towards understanding the infinite subtleties of precisely what the club-going and record buying public would like this week, next week and the week after.

The art of programming consists of the selection and processing of loops (which will require copyright clearance, as will be outlined later) or the creation from scratch of a 'groove'. The importance of the groove in dance music cannot be underestimated.

There are plenty of people who don't really understand the style who hear dance music played on TV (they don't go to clubs, which is why they don't understand) and say, 'I could write a song like that'. Maybe they could, but could they invent the groove to go with it? Creating a groove is easy, creating a groove that sells is not. Perhaps the producer will be a programmer in his own right, or perhaps he will guide and direct a programmer to come up with the foundation that will support the song.

In many cases, MIDI equipment is used not for dance music, but to create music which superficially sounds like it is being played by conventional instruments. The programmer's skill will be applied towards making or selecting the right sounds, not necessarily exact imitations of real instruments, and the producer will have the final say on which sounds are used. Again, much of this work can be done in a home studio and only transferred to a commercial studio at a late stage.

Finally, whether your style of music is sequenced or played live, the process of pre-production is a process of trial and error, where people come up with ideas, try them out, and then the producer selects the best of the bunch that will pass from the rehearsal room into the studio. The next step is to put together the team that will turn a song and a collection of production ideas into a recording.

The producer's home studio

The first rule of home studios is that they are not compulsory! Many musicians have home studios because a good home studio can be much less expensive to operate than to hire even the cheapest and crustiest commercial studio on a regular basis. But if you are working at the highest level of music, then you will have the budget to work in a top studio, and if you are successful you will be doing so regularly. If you work with sequenced music however then you will obviously have your own keyboards and sampler, and a sequencer is an inevitable extra purchase, so effectively you have acquired a studio without really intending to do so.

The question now is how much of this equipment do you want to

The producer's view – Phil Harding

Phil Harding came into production through engineering, from early days at Marquee Studio through to Chief Engineer at Stock, Aitken and Waterman's PWL 'Hit Factory' Studio, and now to production work with keyboard player/programmer partner Ian Curnow.

Assessing the demo

'Demos generally come from managers, publishers and record companies. If someone sends a demo through to us direct then we tend to pass over it, not necessarily because it isn't going to be any good, but we are not really business people. We have never had any success with anyone without a publisher, manager or record company behind them. Our forte is being able to fulfil the potential that an artist has put into their demos, once we have been approached by someone who has the power or money to see it through.'

Developing the demo

'Because Ian and I are writers, we will take something on even if we feel that it needs shaping in a different way, and we will go as far as rewriting it if necessary. There is a fine line between changing an arrangement as a producer so drastically that it becomes a co-writing situation. Many producers end up doing that and are not able to get a co-writing credit because they haven't agreed it with the artist's management beforehand. You can get into all sorts of fights.'

Instrumentation

'We tend to program most of what we do, but we did some production recently with Let Loose and they wanted the final record to have as much live drums and live guitar as possible. We programmed a lot beforehand and combined it with the live drums and guitars, and then sat down with them afterwards to decide how much of the live stuff they wanted to use and how much of the programmed stuff. But generally most of our records are programmed from top to bottom, apart from the vocals obviously.'

transport to a commercial studio once you have sequenced your basic tracks? Bear in mind that taking your whole setup apart and re-erecting it somewhere else isn't a whole load of fun. In this field of music it would be wise to find a well set up studio which you could use, which may be tied to a label and not operating as a commercial studio in the normal sense of the word, and choose equipment similar to theirs. If you have the same sampler and sequencer, you might find that all you need to take with you are a few floppy disks and maybe your source material for loops. The synths might be different models, but it shouldn't be too much trouble to find sounds that fit what you have in mind.

Vocals too?

Since you have the basics of a recording studio at home already then a worthwhile next step could be to record vocals there too. You might just be thinking of trying out a few ideas, or your singer might

The Alesis M20 20-bit ADAT recorder is capable of studio quality recording at home, just add a good mic pre-amp and simple monitor mixer to record vocals

Neumann U87 the world's favourite vocal mic (pic courtesy Sennheiser)

suddenly get the urge to record and it would be wise not to waste their energy and enthusiasm.

To record vocals you need a quiet, dry acoustic, a good microphone (such as that perennial favourite the Neumann U87), and a digital multitrack to which you can synchronise your sequencer. If your mixing console isn't really up to the job then you should buy a rack mounting mic preamplifier. The mic and preamp will cost a bit, but if you are recording vocals at home you shouldn't skimp on cheap equipment. Your equipment must be exactly as good as the equipment in a top studio, even if you don't have as much of it.

If non-sequenced bands are your speciality, then there isn't much point in having a home studio. If it was good enough, then it would have cost so much you would have to open it up for hire to make it pay, and I think you probably want to be a producer rather than a studio manager! This doesn't mean that you can't do some work at home. You may have a digital multitrack and a small mixing console which you can use to compile parts of several vocal takes into one good one. This can be time consuming, and you can probably do it better by yourself in your own surroundings. You may also want to have a computer and sequencer for the odd bit of sequencing that needs to be done, or to prepare click tracks in advance of the recording session.

There are no rules, just consider what is practical and cost effective to do at home, and remember never to lower your standards and do something at home which you could have done better in a proper studio.

The producer's view – Phil Fearon

Phil Fearon has developed from being a successful artist, and probably one of the first serious home studio owners, to being chairman of the Production House dance label, where he now sees his role as an 'executive producer' overseeing the work of others and making sure it is progressing satisfactorily towards a commercially successful release. Baby D's journey towards success started on Production House and they have since moved on to major label status, with Production House maintaining their involvement on the management side.

Assessing the demo

'So many records sound the same and I am straining to find a little bit of originality. Songwriting ability is the greatest thing I look for, and the creative element. We normally only take on writers who can produce and do some kind of engineering. The people we work with tend to have three or four talents all rolled into one.'

Song structure

'I don't get much involved for the club version but when it comes to airplay, that's when I would give my opinion. If it is all beat and no music then that's cool, but if I think that it has to be a little more radio friendly or better for the video then I do get heavily involved to make sure that the main parts are featured in the four minutes. I may throw my weight around but when we are spending big money I want to make sure that it is absolutely correct.'

Understanding the style

'Producers now often come from being DJs. They are out there and they just know what the kids like on the dance floor. It's very useful to know what this week's tempo is, and what it's going to be in a couple of weeks time. It's changing every fortnight, but it's a subtle change and only the DJs have got that on-the-button knowledge.'

'Surround yourself with good people'. That was the secret for success given by one of the biggest selling British recording artists in history, and it's true for producers too. You can try to be a 'one man band' producer, especially since there is an incredible array of equipment available which in theory makes it possible. But when you consider that virtually every record that hits the charts is the joint effort of at least five people then you have to consider the old saying, 'Five heads are better than one'!

Who are these five people, you ask? Well this doesn't apply to every case but a typical example may be a dance track created by an artist, programmer, producer and engineer under the ultimate guidance of the record company's A&R manager. And of course these will all be 'good people' otherwise (a) they wouldn't get a hit, and (b) top professionals only work with other top professionals.

So how can you compete when you are working from your bedroom studio? Is it a lost cause? Well no, but I can't promise you it won't be very very difficult to get your foot in the door. The first step is to accept that you can't go it alone and you need to find other people to work with, to pool your talents and abilities.

The one advantage you have over the top professionals is your creativity. Creativity, that is, in the sense that as a newcomer to the industry you will find your own methods, techniques and, most importantly, sounds. The Top 40 buying public basically demands 'more of the same', but almost always spiced with something new that they haven't heard before. You might have this magic ingredient in abundance where the top pros have used up all of theirs. All you have to do is work out where you want to specialise; as a musician, programmer, engineer or producer and then find other like-minded people as talented as yourself to work with, and go out and make that hit! If you can't find someone to fulfil a particular role, then you will have to pay for the necessary expertise.

There's no shame or stigma in paying a professional musician, engineer or whatever – it just hurts! But you will reap the rewards of knowing that the people you hire are doing their job professionally and allowing you to give your full attention to your own role and perform it to the best of your ability.

The most difficult form of production is trying to take a mediocre band or musician and make them sound good, and I'm afraid this is the route upon which many aspiring producers start off. It may just be the road to nowhere, but on the other hand, some people might find it the tough training ground that they need.

The A&R manager

The A&R manager is certainly a creative person in his or her own right. Out of the thousands of artists, musicians, writers and bands there are around, the A&R manager has to pick the one that is going to be successful, and nurture their career into the big money zone.

The A&R manager is going to be the enabler of success – but only for the chosen few. And out of the few who are chosen to be given the opportunity of fame, fortune and success, many will fall at the first hurdle – their first recording doesn't sell and the record company invokes one of a number of 'get out' clauses in the contract and bids them goodbye.

Among the many who would like to be successful as an solo artist or band, most see that elusive recording contract as their goal. In fact, a recording contract is just an entry into a high stakes game of snakes and ladders where unfortunately the ladders are few, long and steep, and the snakes are many and exceedingly slippery – as any contracted artist turned van driver will tell you!

Many people outside the industry see the A&R department of a record company as a barrier, an obstacle to their success. In fact it is the opposite – the A&R manager is the *enabler* of success, for the chosen few.

Dealing with A&R

As a producer, your dealings with the A&R department of a record company will take one of two forms. Either the record company has signed an act and they approach you to produce it, or you have associated yourself – or even created – an act and you offer it to the company.

Choosing a producer is a key part of the A&R manager's role because the producer can potentially make or break the record. It is usually considered important that the artist or band gets on well with the producer and can work with them comfortably. If there is stress in the studio then it is likely not to be musically productive, although there have been exceptions to this rule.

The band would also have to respect the producer. Many bands have the attitude of 'we know what we are doing and we don't want to be produced', but you just have to look at how many bands have made it big with a producer's assistance, and how many bands haven't got anywhere because they were too pigheaded to relinquish just a little bit of control. The producer of course should also have respect for the band, simply because if he or she doesn't think that the band is any good, then the motivation to do a good piece of work just won't be there.

A&R manager's view – Geoff Travis

Geoff Travis' A&R credits include the Rough Trade and Blanco y Negro labels. He has also been involved in the management of acts including Pulp and The Cranberries.

On Stephen Street

'Stephen Street (producer of the first two Cranberries albums) has a very clear view of what works and what doesn't, but he's not afraid of trying things. He is the kind of person who is there to bring the best out of a band rather than impose his will. He is totally open minded and he is more likely to say, 'That sounds like an interesting idea, let's try it', than he is to say, 'That sounds like a crap idea, why don't you go home and let me get on with it'.'

New producers

'If I didn't know a producer, I would listen to what he had done and then meet him. The same way when you meet an artist, if they talk sense to you and if they have got a kind of spark, I give them a try. The band need to feel comfortable with them, they are the ones doing the work.'

Listening to work in progress

'I like to go to the studio and see what's happening. Some bands invite you to make comments and want to get feedback. Other people just want to get on with it. I don't try to impose and interfere, unless there was something drastically wrong. My experience of bands is that the better the band, the more they know what they want.'

The producer's track record

Often the A&R manager will look at a producer's track record. If a producer has a history of success with guitar orientated bands, then it would be a safe option to choose him to produce your newly signed guitar band. If a producer has had dance floor success, then he could be exactly right for your new solo artist. It's the 'horses for courses' principle. But there's a little more to it than that. Perhaps a band has already done an album and achieved moderate success, enough success to be allowed to do a second. If you were the A&R manager would you choose the same producer?

Perhaps if the producer was new to the business and you thought he may be capable of greater achievement then you may choose the same person again. But if the first album had been produced by an established name, then you would start to consider why it had only been a moderate rather than a stunning success. Of course, you could put it down to the way the act had been marketed, but let's concentrate on the musical side of things.

Since the album did sell, then there must have been something good about it, so the trick would be to choose a producer who can

A&R manager's view – David Bates

David Bates' A&R credits include Mercury and Polygram, working with many acts ranging from Oleta Adams to Definition of Sound.

Choosing a producer
'You wouldn't necessarily put Oleta Adams with a heavy metal producer, but if the safe option is busy then sometimes you try a more adventurous choice. I work with Chris Hughes a lot and he has produced people like Paul McCartney and Tears for Fears. I put him with Definition of Sound (*Pass the Vibes* was a successful single for them) because they wanted to be different and not forced into a rap mould.'

Budgeting
'Not cutting off creativity to meet a deadline is one of my weaknesses in the eyes of the accountants. I don't try and make something fit into a budget, I try to make the best record I can. You only get one shot at a record. If you had an idea you wanted to try and you didn't, and then the record didn't chart you would be cursing yourself.'

If there's no obvious single on the album
'We spent a year with Lloyd Cole, getting him to try and write a single with different people but it just didn't work. Having done that we said, 'Let's just mix the record and see if there's a track that stands out'. Suddenly this track *Like Lovers Do* began to stand out. It was Lloyd's first hit in nine years!'

replicate all of those good things, and add even more to the band's sound, songs or performance. This was the case with the Pulp album, *Different Class*. Pulp's management, who handled this aspect of the A&R role, decided that although they had been pleased with Pulp's previous album, certain elements had been missed. They felt that there was a richness and depth to their live sound which hadn't been fully captured. Chris Thomas was engaged to produce the record and the subsequent success of this album confirmed that he was the right man for the job.

Tying up with a band
Alternatively, you might start your career as a producer by associating yourself with a band, developing and recording them, and then presenting them to a record company. This is a slightly risky business because the record company might say that they like the band but they don't like you! If you have done the groundwork properly then you won't be too upset because you will have drawn up an agreement with the band so that you receive a payoff, or at least reimbursement of any costs you have incurred.

A&R people I have spoken to confirm that this is a viable approach, but you do have to present an 'act', and not just a recording. A band that can play live is an act, for example, and so is a solo singer with obvious sex appeal. Other than that, you will have to find an angle that the record company can use to market the material you produce.

Marketing and A&R

The A&R manager's role certainly doesn't finish with finding bands and choosing producers – that is where it begins. The A&R manager will nurture the creative team all the way through the recording process. The producer's skill will be in creating great music, or at least assisting the creation of great music. The A&R manager understands what sells – and I'm sure you are well aware that there is a lot of great music about that hasn't sold nearly as much as it seems to deserve. Some A&R managers rely on their instincts to make a good choice of producer and then let them get on with it with little or no interference, unless it seems that there is something going seriously wrong in some way.

One thing that might go wrong is that a whole album is recorded and there isn't an obvious single on it. For many acts, singles are a vital marketing tool without which the album cannot be a success. In this case the A&R manager will either get the band to write some more songs, re-record one of the songs with more attention given to its singles chart potential, release one of the album tracks as a single and hope for the best, or if the worst comes to the worst scrap the whole project! This last situation is one you would probably prefer to avoid because you'll find yourself on the scrapheap too.

The engineer

Producers who started their careers as engineers are obviously perfectly capable of doing the engineering themselves, and some do. In a decent studio, there will be an assistant engineer available to handle all the menial tasks of setting up mic stands and plugging in cables, so the producer will be able to concentrate on getting a good sound whenever he wears his engineer's hat. The problem with this arrangement is that being a great engineer is a very difficult and demanding job, and so is being a producer. Anyone who can fulfil both roles 100% is obviously some kind of genius, and I don't deny that some producers are.

There are also many producers who probably wouldn't know what a knob was, let alone know how to twiddle it, so obviously an engineer is necessary, and not just the studio junior taking a break from his coffee making duties either. With a first class engineer at the desk, a musically orientated producer can concentrate fully on

You might think that the producer takes a superior position to the engineer and tells him what to do, but where top professionals are involved this is unlikely to be the case.

Engineer's view – Gregg Jackman

Gregg Jackman is a very well established and respected engineer, and is one of the few engineers who can command royalties on his recordings rather than just a flat fee.

On working with a top producer

'The Seal album took a very long time. Trevor Horn doesn't worry too much about the time it takes or the budget. He just wants to make a great record. Sometimes when you think you are getting somewhere it can be scrapped and started all over again. 'Now I know how to make this record. Wipe it and we'll start again'. You learn not to take any of these things personally.'

Discussions with the producer

'Very often people will ask me my opinion. As long as they are prepared to accept that I may say something they don't like, that's fine. Producers tend to observe what it sounds like. Sometimes they'll point out something you haven't heard. They'll say, 'The vocals sound a bit toppy' when you are worrying about the bass guitar and you haven't noticed it. It's good to have two sets of ears concentrating on the job in hand.'

Styles of production

'Some producers don't know anything about sound. They are just very good musicians, good at sorting out arrangements. As long as there isn't something terribly wrong with it they hardly ever seem to comment about the sound. Having said that, there are many more technical producers than there used to be.'

creating a good arrangement and maximising the potential of the performance while the engineer deals with the sound.

The engineer may take a couple of hours getting a drum kit sound while the producer occasionally listens, talks to the other members of the band, makes phone calls, drinks coffee and paces up and down a bit. Unless he has very specific requirements, he will trust the engineer's judgment, and the only comment he may make is, 'OK – it's good enough now, let's start recording!'. Engineers, being dedicated to achieving the ultimate in recorded sound, sometimes don't know when to stop!

The engineer/producer

One problem about being an engineer/producer is that you have no-one to ask what they think about something. You could ask a member of the band, to which the reply would probably be, 'I don't know, you're meant to be the producer'. Having an engineer as a sounding board for your ideas and opinions is a great help because you can rely on a good engineer being able to give you good advice, and they will probably have the psychological skills to know when to disagree with you openly, and when to give you the answer you are looking for, regardless of what they really think.

An established engineer may even suggest to you that something isn't working well musically. You may regard this as an intrusion into your role, but you would be unwise not to pay attention to the advice of someone who has probably worked on literally thousands of sessions and, without being able to play an instrument or sing a note, has almost certainly achieved an understanding of music equal – perhaps superior – to your own.

If, as a producer, you don't have any engineering knowledge or skills to speak of, then at the very least you should develop an awareness of what the engineer can do for you, what tricks and techniques the engineer can employ, and gain a feeling for how long something you ask for may take to set up or perform.

One of the worst things that will happen to an engineer is for a producer to bring in a demo cassette and say, 'I want it to sound like this'. This situation isn't as common as it used to be, but it is still very easy for a musician to be working in his or her home studio and come upon a particular sound just by chance, which they then develop into a major feature of the song. The problems may be: that the song structure may change, the key may change, or the multitrack tape of the demo may be of poor quality or may have been lost.

Any of these factors will mean that the sound will have to be recreated somehow, and anyone who has any experience of this will tell you that it is sometimes very very difficult. You may have to accept that it could take a long time to work out how the sound was achieved, unless the musician concerned has a very good memory, or you may have to settle for a near alternative. Of course, you won't settle for second best, but sometimes trying to recreate a sound – sometimes the sound of another artist's work – may prove impossible, but along the way you will stumble upon something equally interesting or even better that you would not have thought of if you had just started from scratch.

Mixing

At the mixing stage, producers often just leave the engineer to get on with it in his or her own time. You might have thought that if the producer is supposed to be in charge of the recording, then he or she should supervise every aspect of the recording process, including every detail of the mixing. Of course, any engineer will tell you that you do have to be an engineer to appreciate fully the subtle art of mixing. Having a producer in the studio in the early stages of mixing would only be inhibiting. If the engineer is left to his own devices for two or three hours, then the producer can come in and apply his fresh ears to the mix and comment on what is going well, what isn't working etc.

There is a balance to be made between how much the engineer will stick to what's on the tape and how much he will alter the sound of the individual tracks with EQ and effects. I'll have more to say about this later.

*I*n the previous chapter I explained how record production is a team effort, with the record producer in the role of team leader, with the record company's A&R manager having the absolute final say. In some types of production, the rest of the team consists of the band, and no-one else need be involved. But for a solo artist, there has to be a musical backing of some sort, and unless he or she happens to be an extremely talented multi-instrumentalist (or the producer is), then extra musical input will be necessary.

The arranger

Before samplers and synthesisers were quite as all-singing and all-dancing as they are now, arrangers were commonly employed to put the music together and work with a number of session musicians to create a musical backing in a style appropriate for the song. Now, many programmers and keyboard players effectively take on the arranger's role themselves, for the simple reason that a few modules, and a few CD-ROMs perhaps, can supply just about any instrumental sound that could possibly be required, and all you have to do is play the notes into a sequencer and you have an 'instant' arrangement.

Of course, even though an arranger may no longer be necessary, good arrangements for synths and samplers don't create themselves automatically, so this is no easy option. For certain styles of music, arrangers are still used. For example, it is difficult to get the best out of a string section, brass section or orchestra, unless you have a deep understanding of the instruments, and the way in which they interact. You could bash out a few chords on a keyboard, get your favourite sequencer software to turn them into musical dots, and hand them out to a group of string players. But would it get the best out of the players and the instruments? I think not.

Types of arranger

Arrangers seem to come in two types, lone arrangers (I think there's a pun in there somewhere!) who work at home with a sharpened pencil and large sheets of music manuscript paper, and arrangers who are themselves members of a string or horn section. I could also

Arranger's view – John Altman

Credits include Bjork's *It's Oh So Quiet*, Alison Moyet's *That Old Devil Called Love*, Simple Minds' *Street Fighting Years* and Monty Python's *Always Look On the Bright Side of Life*.

On types of producer

'Some producers are very specific about sounds and styles of writing. They will go over the arrangements they want with you quite meticulously. Other producers will ask you to do what you feel is right, and then on the session you will take out a phrase, repeat a couple of bars or something like that. In a lot of cases people ask for me because they know what I can do, and I get a free hand to go in any direction I want.'

Writing the dots

'I don't have a computer or a synthesiser. I find writing out music is quicker than doing it on a computer. I wrote and orchestrated the tank chase sequence in *Goldeneye* in about half a day. Once you get the momentum you can just hear what the strings and brass ought to be doing. Technology just gets in the way.'

On working with George Michael

'He wanted input from the ground up on *Kissing a Fool*. At a certain point he took over and what became of it was his take on what I had done. He has a very precise ear and he knows what he wants. I thoroughly enjoy working with him'

put backing vocalists into this category too since a trio of singers can often work out their own vocal arrangements, saving the producer a job. You will recognise the occasion when you need to hire an arranger when someone says, 'I think we need an orchestra on this track', or a jazz band, big band or even choir. Your first port of call will be your CD collection where you will scan through discs where you remember a song being given the orchestral treatment, and hopefully the arranger will be credited in the booklet. A call to the Musicians' Union will probably get the two of you in touch. Likewise, you may find that string and horn sections are credited on the CDs on which they appear and you might even find them in the phone book or Yellow Pages.

Of course, I have to say that London is still the centre of musical activity in the UK, and you will stand a better chance of finding the arrangers and musicians you have heard of in the metropolis. If you live elsewhere in the country, you will still be able to find excellent musicians and arrangers, but you might not be able to expect them to have as much experience in recording.

For a larger group of instruments, the musical director or MD might wear the headphones and conduct the musicians. If the MD

String players very often find studio recording much more difficult than playing live. The reason is that if they have to wear headphones, they won't be able to hear themselves in the way they are used to and they will inevitably find keeping in tune more difficult.

Arranger's view – Wil Malone

Wil Malone's credits include Peter Gabriel, Depeche Mode, Massive Attack, Seal, Neneh Cherry and Simple Minds.

On numbers of string players
'Sometimes 10, sometimes 40. It's about texture, warmth and a lot of different things. If a producer says to me, 'I want this to sound very big but I have only so much money', then there's a problem.'

Supporting the vocals
'I am working on a project with a girl singer which is just orchestra with no rhythm section. Her voice is slightly thinnish so I have added violas into the string arrangement just to pick up the lower range of her voice to bring out the bottom edge. That is the kind of thinking behind what I do.'

Changing the arrangement in the studio
'I rewrite it for the principal of each section and ask them to pass it on. It's the quickest way I've found. It happens quite a lot since you often get a track where the vocalist has changed his phrasing and you need to make adjustments.'

doesn't have much recording experience, he may find it difficult getting the musicians to keep pace with a totally inflexible previously recorded backing track.

Session musicians

Once upon a time it was every instrumentalist's dream to become a session musician. With the unstoppable rise of computerised instruments, the demand for session players has diminished, but there is still a keen market at the top of the business. The reason you would hire a specialist session musician rather than use your mate who can pick and strum a bit is simply because a good session musician can project a wonderful air of confidence into the recording.

As your experience as a producer increases you will find that there is a world of difference between someone who can play well, and someone who really 'has it' – 'it' being that indefinable something that makes a recording sound terrific rather than just all right.

You shouldn't experience problems if you get your musicians from a reputable source who is used to dealing with top producers. This source would be what used to be called a 'fixer', nowadays more politely known as a session agent or orchestral contractor. Whatever instrument or voice you need, you can ring up a session agent and he or she will be able to deliver the goods – at a price.

If you want quality, then you can forget about Musicians' Union rates, because these are considered to be a bare minimum level of remuneration. Of course, when the payment tops the MU scale, then

Be warned that there is still a breed of session musician that thinks it is OK to place a copy of *Autotrader* on the music stand and imagine that they are professional enough not to have to give their full attention to what they are doing. I would personally show someone the door if they did this, but I'm afraid it is still considered to be acceptable practice in some circles.

you will also get flexibility and a certain amount of freedom from MU conditions on how sessions are conducted. You would need to clarify these points with the contractor and find out precisely what you are agreeing to in terms of the duration of the session, breaks, maximum recording time etc. Be prepared to sign a contract or letter of agreement which will also contain the performers' consent required under the Copyright, Designs and Patents Act for the types of use proposed for the recording.

Bear in mind that not all the musicians on a session agent's books will have reached the pinnacle of their careers. Some will just be starting out, and although the agent will have taken them on because they have outstanding ability, they may need to build up a track record and could see your project as a means to this end, at least in part.

But what if your budget is limited, or you only want to make a demo recording and can't justify too much expense? One possibility is that you can interest a top session player sufficiently to work for you for the minimum fee simply because they like the music. Admittedly, this is easier if the session player knows you already, but certainly not impossible since musicians like to play, and if they like your music they will probably want to play it.

Another strategy is to book a musician on a demo rate which may be lower than a full session rate. Of course, you won't be able to release the recordings since you will never be allowed to book a session player again if you do. But you could record your demo, hawk it around the record companies, and if someone does take to it and wants to release it, all you have to do is go back to the session agent and renegotiate the fee. You can't lose!

Musician's view – Andy Duncan

As a drummer/rhythm programmer Andy's credits include Take That, Tina Turner, The Beautiful South and the Manic Street Preachers.

Getting work
'It's all word of mouth recommendation. Agencies try very hard to represent musicians, often fruitlessly because recording is a high cost, high pressure enterprise and no-one wants to recommend someone who is going to make a fool of them. Producers generally are very wary of using people that they have never heard of because they don't know what they are going to get when the person walks in through the door.'

What the producer asks of a session musician
'All producers have their own methods, but most of

the people I work with regularly call me in to be creative. They don't just call me in to play an idea that they have got. I have worked quite a lot with Trevor Horn over the years and I said to him that my enjoyment was in being presented with a rhythmic puzzle that I have to solve. He said that that's the same way he feels about producing, except that he is solving the entire musical puzzle, not just a segment of it.'

Fees
'I got into music because I love music, not because I want to make loads of money. I have a ludicrously expensive rate I go out for, but if something sounds like really great fun, I'm quite happy to be negotiable. I often think I'm a very lucky person to be doing this. I'm getting paid to do the thing I would most love to do anyway.'

Musician's view – Dave Clayton

Keyboard player Dave Clayton's credits include Take That album producer Chris Porter. He also played on George Michael's *Jesus to a Child*.

Equipment

'I tend to bring it all, leave it in a room somewhere and bring out what I need. I've got masses of analogue gear and modern equipment too – clavinets and electric pianos, Roland System 100 up to the new Waldorf Wave.'

Producers' requirements

'Some get me in to show them how it could be. They rely on my experience and see if I can develop something from their idea. They might like the sound of a particular era and just let me jam and find a way I can fuse it into their track.'

Fees

'I've had people quote MU rates to me, but people hire me because of my ability and also because of the fact that I can bring in a lot of equipment as well. The rate varies from project to project. I might work for someone on a small label for a negligible rate and charge the full rate to people who can afford it. I'm in the fortunate position that I've been in the business a few years and I tend to do things I feel will inspire me.'

Session musician Dave Clayton at work in producer Chris Parker's private studio

Session agent's view – Debbie Haxton

Debbie Haxton runs the Session Connection session agency who handle many of the top musicians in the UK.

Choosing the right people

'Quite often there will be eight or nine people who can do the gig, and one of them will be the absolute right one. We take pride in what we put together. We want producers to be very very happy with the people we send. 99% of the time it works out well.'

Fees

'For a lead vocal we ask for an advance and then points. A lead vocal is going to make or break the track, and if it does make it then the vocalist should be getting royalties, somewhere between two to five percent for a first single. If there is a band who wants a guitarist and they can't pay very much, I'll put them in touch with one of the younger people on the books and say if you want to go ahead just do it. Sometimes there's no point in getting involved except to get the younger people started. We can put people in touch with each other and sort of try and create families.'

Talking to the Kick Horns

The Kick Horns are Simon Clarke (alto and baritone sax, flute), Roddy Lorimer (trumpet and flugelhorn) and Tim Sanders (tenor and soprano sax). Credits include Blur, The Rolling Stones, Rod Stewart, Eric Clapton, The Stereo MCs and Trevor Horn.

Do you use additional musicians if necessary?

We do use additional musicians when the music requires it and if the budget allows, most often trombone and/or extra trumpet. On Blur's *Modern Life is Rubbish*, one track (*Sunday Sunday*) called for brass band instruments such as the euphonium and tenor horn, while Chris Rea (on *Auberge*) asked for an eight-piece section: two trumpets, two saxes, two trombones, bass trombone and tuba.

Our favourite big section line-up, and the most versatile, is two trumpets, two saxes and trombone. Touring with The Who in 1989 required this sound, and more recently *African Woman* on Baaba Maal's *Firin' in Fouta* album. On the Rolling Stones's *Steel*

Wheels we worked as a four-piece, adding an extra trumpet to give more bite to the sound; and on *Hang on St. Christopher*, recorded for Rod Stewart's *A Spanner in the Works*, trombone brought mid-range attack and rudeness to the voicings.

We can also 'cheat' by double-tracking, but generally we prefer the sound of musicians playing together in one room at the same time.

Where would a producer find out about you?

Contacts are made almost always by word of mouth. We used to be in Yellow Pages, but we don't do weddings and Roddy found it hard to keep a straight face when callers asked for 'Mr Horns' or 'Kick'.

Do you expect to come into the studio and find parts already written out for you?

It's only rarely that we're given other people's arrangements to play – but we're very happy to play them, then come away having learnt some new ideas!

Talking to the Kick Horns (cont)

More often, especially on Japanese sessions for some reason, we have been given a score from which to work out our own voicings and, most importantly, phrasings.

Can you make up arrangements yourselves in the studio?

We're very keen on pre-production meetings as they give us a chance to get to know the artist and producer before we work together, as well as allowing us some time to get to know the music and, ideally, come up with the definitive horn arrangement – which may well change in the studio... On the other hand, there are occasions when our job is so straightforward, or so clearly dictated by the artist or producer, that pre-production would merely waste time.

When we worked on *Connected* for the Stereo MCs they had no songs, just various grooves they were working on. Rob sang horn lines to us very quietly, which we then tried on different instruments, with a variety of harmonies and phrasings, recording 30 second bursts or riffs. They then put the record together like a four-dimensional jigsaw.

In the studio with Eric Clapton, the entire band recording live, no overdubs, no repairs. One morning Eric suggested covering Lowell Fulson's *Sinner's Prayer*. We all listened to the Ray Charles version in the control room a few times, then walked straight back into the studio to record it in about three takes. I guess Eric had done some homework, but it was new to the rest of us.

We spent Christmas 1984 on the China Crisis *Flaunt the Imperfection* with Walter Becker. He gave us printouts of the top-line melodies, and then auditioned all kinds of harmonies and voicings, for example, trumpet below flute below soprano sax with trombone on top, unusual but beautiful sounds which Walter recorded straight down to a stereo pair when he heard the blend just right. He had the most incredible ears – and patience.

How long would it take to arrange and record the horn section on the average song (if there is such as thing)?

For one song, a three-hour session is usually plenty of time, and we would reckon on recording three to four songs in a day.

Beyond average

With Trevor Horn, recording *Hang on to St. Christopher*, after one run-through: 'The parts sound great to me – please record them with the engineer and call me when you've finished.' We did, and an hour and a half later he smiled and we left.

Talking to the Kick Horns (cont)

We recorded *Goodbye Sally* for Carmel, starting at noon on what we knew would be a tough blow, especially for Roddy. Horrendous maintenance problems lost us six hours of studio time, the desk shedding channels like milk-teeth, and at 2 a.m. we were still doing overdubs. Despite everyone's tiredness, producer Hugh Jones got a fabulous sound on tape, firing everyone up with his honest excitement and enthusiasm to give of their best.

On our first session for Gary Langan for the band Pele, a live sort of approach was asked for. So we recorded fast, six songs in two sessions with the three of us adding harmonies on a double track. This was only possible because thorough pre-production left us with only a tweak of fine tuning to do to the arrangements.

Arranging, whether at home or on the spot, is the most time consuming part of the process as it involves a complex series of decisions and collaborations. When we do more than a couple of takes of something it's often not because we haven't played a phrase right, but because the bass player wants to hear a big chord with a fall on the end, while the singer wants us to play a unison line that the keyboard player hates, and the producer has earmarked for backing vocals. We meanwhile tend to think we should play nothing at this point so as not to preempt the swell before the chorus!

What would a producer typically ask of you?

At one extreme, our brief could be to replace a synth guide part with real horns as faithfully as possible; at the other it could be: 'You guys would be great on this track. You know the kind of thing.' Typically, it's somewhere in between. We'll meet the producer before the session, listen to the songs, make a note of any specific melody lines required, discuss stylistic reference points, line-up etc. Then we go away and write the arrangements, trying to make the horns work as well as possible within the brief we've been given.

Would a producer ask you to change what you are playing?

Sometimes a producer will change not a single note, and sometimes ideas change during the recording process, or new ones pop up out of the ether as we play, or the track has moved on since our pre-production meeting. Whatever the reason, it is always possible to make other ideas work. Indeed, this can be a lot of fun, and we're not in the least precious about ditching our original thoughts.

Do you have any influence on the way the engineer sets up the mics?

As fellow professionals, engineers are as concerned to get things right as we are, and usually welcome our suggestions. We like to spend a few minutes listening and checking that we're on the right mics at the right distance for the acoustic of the room and that balances etc. go to tape correctly. This can save a lot of time and trouble later.

Thankfully, most engineers nowadays are keen to get a good natural sound on tape, so we rarely encounter over-compression or unnecessary EQ knob twiddling. But there were dark corners of the eighties when even the music press seemed mesmerised by the electro bleep. In 1985, the Melody Maker review of the Waterboys' *The Whole of the Moon* gallingly referred to Roddy's majestic trumpet instrumental as 'fantastic synth sounds'.

Do you normally finish a song in one session?

Yes

How much do you charge?

We charge a reasonable rate, either by the three-hour session or by the day, for our time in the studio, but pre-production and arranging incur no extra cost as we like to encourage this part of the process. Our session rate is marginally higher than the MU's double tracking rate.

Talking to the Kick Horns (cont)

Do you stick to MU rules about session duration, amount of recording time, breaks etc?

We regard ourselves as a small band, and as such go into the studio to work at the pace and in the way that suits the music and the people. If we need a break or a cup of tea we just ask for it. On the other hand there have been times when, anxious to drop in a phrase on the third chorus, we've peered expectantly at the dim and distant control-room window only to find that the engineer has gone for a pee and the producer is on the phone to his architect. These MU rules are needed in sessions involving large numbers of players but are not really relevant to our situation.

What advantages would a producer get from booking the Kick Horns rather than individual musicians?

A producer booking individual musicians gets just that, whereas with the Kick Horns he would get a very efficient horn section with a shared blend, feel and sense of phrasing achieved by thirteen years of playing together. He would get a team with a long-standing commitment to the song and the singer, who enjoy collaboration with the band and the producer, who understand each other, whose aim is quite simply to make the song sound better.

The programmer

There is a very subtle dividing line between keyboard players and programmers. Let's say that a keyboard player specialises in tinkling the keys and may tweak the odd sound here and there if he feels inclined, whereas a programmer is hired for his collection of instruments, sounds and samples, and is expect to be able to produce exactly the right sound for the occasion, and maybe do a bit of playing on the side.

Programmer Steve McNichol working with engineer Paul Gomersall

Programmer's view – Steve McNichol

Among many other credits, Steve McNichol was the programmer on George Michael's *Older*.

Working with the producer

'I think it's important when programmers work with producers or artists, to be able to work together in a similar way. I've been in a situation where people have had an idea in their head and they have explained it to me, and my understanding of it was different to theirs. If you are on a similar wavelength you can get things done a bit quicker. It's also a matter of learning to understand how they describe things. It's the age old thing, a producer might say, 'Make it brighter'. Your reaction might be to crank the top end up, but that might not be what he means. One producer's description may be completely different to another's. You almost have to be able to read their minds.'

As a budding producer, perhaps you have a MIDI setup and are capable of programming yourself, as many established producers are. But you will be aware that programming takes a lot of mental energy and patience. Hiring a programmer to do something that perhaps you could have expended valuable energy on yourself will allow you to concentrate fully on the music, which is exactly what a producer needs to do. The programmer will also have a fantastic memory for sounds, and when you need a string sound that is just so, the programmer will be able to call up a few patches and demonstrate them to you so that you can choose the best.

Equipment-wise, what should you expect a programmer to bring to the session? Having seen top programmers in action, I can say that you should be expecting three or four keyboards, a couple of racks full of modules, a powerful computer equipped with a pair of large monitors running an audio sequencer and Digidesign Pro Tools, and all the interfaces disks, cables, backup devices etc that are necessary to make it all work.

The time spent setting up such a system is considerable, as is the time spent after each day's work logging all the sounds and making sure that they can be recalled the next day, or at any later time, if necessary. It is quite common for a producer to regard a programmer as a kind of producer's assistant. The producer will give the programmer an idea of what he wants, then go away for an hour or two and leave the programmer alone with the equipment to see what he can come up with. This is where you really need to be working with people who understand your requirements and who you can trust to come up with something that is likely to suit your taste.

5 Choosing a studio

As a top record producer you will be booking into a top studio. A top studio will of course charge a top price, but since the record company is paying the bill (and charging it to the band's future royalties), all you have to do is make sure you come out with a chart topping record.

As an aspiring producer still working your way up the ladder of success, your budget will be more limited, perhaps to what you yourself can afford, so you will have to be very careful in your choice of studio and arrive at the best compromise between doing certain tasks in the comfort of your home studio, and watching the clock ticking in a good commercial studio at around a penny a second, or more.

Commercial studios can be split fairly arbitrarily into three types: demo studios, mid range, and cost-no-object. Let's take a look at what you will get from each of these three types of studio:

Demo studio

No studio owner will describe their facility as a demo studio, but at the lower end of the price range you will encounter compromises that will reduce the likelihood of being able to make a top quality recording.

Some demo studios have a general air of crustiness. They obviously don't employ cleaners on a regular basis, the staff are miserable and surly, the equipment though once good is now falling apart and you or your engineer have to work around dead channels and dodgy patchbay connections. If you think I'm joking, I'm not. I have a lot of respect for anyone who can make money out of operating a recording studio, such is the competition, but there surely must be a marketing opportunity for a studio that can provide a clean efficient working environment at a reasonably low cost. To be on the safe side, you would need to look at the upper division of demo studios to have a reasonable degree of confidence that you will be able to get good quality work done.

Mid range studio

Moving into the mid range league of studios, what you will tend to find is a studio that was once very well set up, but is now looking rather tired, both in terms of equipment and decor. Decor may not be important to you if you can live with torn carpets, lumpy sofas, and equipment which is ten to fifteen years old, and looks it. But as long as the equipment is well maintained, then it doesn't matter how knocked about it appears, nor how old it is within reason.

Just as you will feel comfortable in your old worn out jeans and trainers, then an old, worn out studio (but with good equipment maintenance) may be just right for you.

If you don't need an awe inspiring environment to do your best work, you can make a great recording in a mid price studio – as top producers continue to prove. There is also something to be said for a slightly down-market atmosphere, in that it doesn't put pressure on you or the performers. For many styles of music, you need to be totally relaxed and comfortable within your surroundings to perform at your best.

Top rate studio

If you are working with a top act, then undoubtedly you will want to work in a first rate studio. If you imagine a well respected American artist flying first class and being pampered by flight attendants all the way from Los Angeles to the UK, checking into a good five star hotel then settling down for the night after a meal in the restaurant and drinks in the bar. When they go to work (by limo) the next day, they don't want to be downgraded into a two star studio! They are used to the best, and even if they don't demand unreasonable luxury they expect a good business class hotel to offer clean, pleasant surroundings with attentive staff. If there are any problems they should be dealt with quickly and efficiently. A guest expects to be treated politely and with respect.

A good studio should be like a five star hotel, with recording facilities instead of a swimming pool. The food should be good too. The control room will have coffee and tea on tap, courtesy of the tape op or assistant engineer, perhaps a continuously replenished fruit bowl. There should be good quality food available in the studio's bar or restaurant, or these facilities should be very close by. Of course, you have to remember that you are there to work, not to have fun, so don't overdo it!

Mid range and top studios should have good acoustics. What you want from a studio's acoustics is a debatable matter, but you will be looking for freedom from outside noise, a pleasant acoustic environment to perform and record in and an accurate control room for judging the mix.

Some studios specialise in mixing and have only limited recording space, or none at all. The 'sound' of a studio is an important factor, and it is not unknown for producers to use studios on both sides of the Atlantic on a single project because they have distinctive sounds that suit certain instruments, or combinations of instruments, well. Also consider the physical size of the studio. If you have 30 string players to accommodate, you need plenty of elbow-room!

Equipment

Choosing the mixing console

Frequently, the selection of a studio will be governed by the equipment that the producer or engineer requires. Even the record company, if they have become aware that a lot of hits are being made using a particular mixing console, will start to think that some of the magic might rub off. As far as the choice of mixing consoles goes, there are just three: SSL, AMS-Neve or … something else.

SSL SL4000G Plus mixing console at Town House Studios, London

SSL and AMS-Neve still seem to be front runners and other manufacturers' consoles, good though they may be, just haven't been able to find the same status, although Euphonix consoles do seem to be acquiring sufficient popularity to put them among the front runners soon. The reason why AMS-Neve is so popular is that the company has been active since the early 1960s and they have made consistently excellent products with hardly a glitch. This kind of track record has made AMS-Neve a number 1 name, and if you are recording in a studio with an AMS-Neve V series console, then you have no excuse for not getting it right!

SSL haven't been going for quite as long as AMS-Neve, but they made an important breakthrough in console design in what was

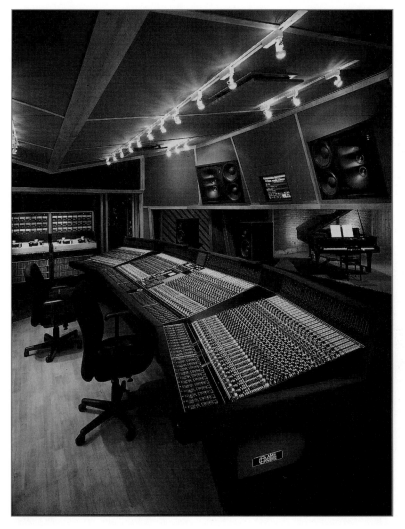

96 channel AMS-Neve VX mixing console at Right Track Recording, New York.

practically their first product. The breakthrough was to incorporate a computer into the console which could control the multitrack remotely and automate the mix. Studios liked it, bought it, and suddenly it seemed like hit after hit was produced on SSL consoles, and the momentum the company gained was massive.

These days, a producer will choose an AMS-Neve studio because, 'I like the sound of Neve'. Another producer will choose SSL because he started off as an engineer on SSL and that is what he is most comfortable with. Judging from the comments of people I have spoken to, there isn't a lot of crossover between the two consoles, you like one or the other, although you will find the occasional producer who will record on AMS-Neve and mix on SSL to get the best of both worlds.

If AMS-Neve and SSL are joint top of the console league table, can you make a hit on any other console? Of course you can. Pick a studio with a top of the range Amek, DDA, Euphonix, Focusrite, Soundcraft, Soundtracs or Trident (in no particular order) and you are almost certain to be perfectly contented since all these consoles and others have made hits, just not as many as AMS-Neve or SSL.

Which multitrack?
Parallel to the choice of console is the choice of multitrack format. It is just as important, but you have more flexibility since you can hire any multitrack you like and bring it into the studio of your choice. Mixing consoles in comparison are very firmly fixed assets. As a top

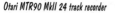
Otari MTR90 MkII 24 track recorder

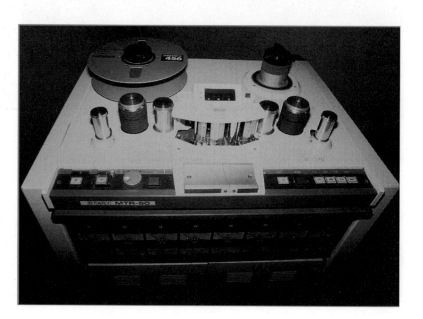

producer, you will be choosing from four formats: 24 track analogue, 24 or 48 track DASH digital, ProDigi 32 track digital or Otari Radar.

It seems that ADAT, DA88 and Pro Tools haven't made it into the top league yet as a main recording medium, although they are often used as a component in the recording process. 24 track analogue machines are still very popular, probably because all the major studios have them already and the damned things just won't wear out. It seems that a properly maintained 24 track can go on just about forever. Many producers still prefer the sound of analogue tape, so I suspect that 24 track machines will be around for decades to come. Whether or not manufacturers will continue to make new ones would be a good question.

King of the 24 tracks is probably the Studer A800, with the Otari MTR90 MkII next in line. The A800 is not a current model, and you could argue that the more recent Studer models are better, but A800s are all around and people love them. Synchronise two of them together and you have 46 tracks worth of pure analogue magic (you lose a track on each for sync) and they will probably be included in the basic rate of the studio. Remember to budget for lots of tape. £300's worth of tape (two reels for 46 track) lasts just over 15 minutes at 30 inches per second!

Maison Rouge Studio set up for Stephen Street. Note the Studer A800 multitrack recorder

If you have a little more money to spend, then you might look at the DASH format. Sony and Studer make DASH machines although the Sonys are far more common. The 3324A is the model you will see most often and for certain styles of music it is considered to be a workhorse machine. People who know Sony DASH machines speak very highly of them and the premium you will pay to have one on your session (even if the studio owns it, usually) will be worthwhile.

Although Mitsubishi pulled out of the digital audio market several years ago, there are still many 32 track ProDigi machines around which will be worked until they drop. In our home and project studios we often fall into the trap of always chasing the latest gear. In pro studios, 'tried and tested' is more often the motto. ProDigi isn't perfect, but many well respected artists and producers are happy to work with it.

The producer's view – Stephen Street

Stephen Street is a producer with both a musical and an engineering background. Bands he has produced include The Smiths, Blur, The Cranberries and Catatonia.

Choosing a studio
'Initially, the main thing is that it has got to sound right. I have to be able to put up a mix or something that I have done and be happy with the way it sounds in the control room. There has got to be a good playing area for the band to record in. You have to capture people at the peak of their performance. They have to be relaxed and in a good frame of mind. You want something that is conducive to that kind of session, so for me it's a good well arranged control room where I can set up a few bits of gear that I take round with me. I want a little bit of space but I'm not a great lover of huge control rooms. There was a time when a lot of studios were building huge control rooms and tiny little playing areas and I am not very keen on that.'

Acoustics
'I prefer wood rooms to stone rooms. Although having said that, I have been using Maison Rouge for the last few years and that has a stone room, but I have been pressing them to try and put some wood down.'

Equipment
'It's is nice to have a good selection but it is not the main thing for me, the main thing for me is a well maintained desk, well maintained machines and good sounding speakers.'

Hard disk recording
The other multitrack recorder I have mentioned isn't a tape recorder – but it thinks it is! Eventually I am sure that hard disk recording will be the norm, but studios still view it with a great deal of caution. The Otari Radar 24 track hard disk recorder however is breaking down barriers. You will probably have to hire it in specially, but you will find that it has the simplicity of tape with the editing capability of hard disk. If you need more tracks, hire two!

Other kit

Aside from the mixing console and the multitrack, everything else is pretty much the icing on the cake. But you would expect a well set up studio to have a good mic selection, a well stocked outboard rack, a grand piano, maybe the odd MIDI keyboard and sampler if you are lucky, and an assistant engineer to help you out with all those knobs and buttons!

I have mentioned maintenance already, because it is vitally important. Also important is the line up of the equipment. Analogue recorders need regular alignment, ideally for each session, to perform at their best, certainly if you plan on recording some instruments in one studio then taking the tape elsewhere for further work. It also helps if the assistant engineer zeros the console by setting every switch and every knob to a neutral position, making it a blank sheet of paper on which you will paint your sound picture.

Stephen Street at Maison Rouge Studio

Booking the studio

Although you can book for shorter periods, it is common to book studios by the day. A 'day' will be around 14 hours, which means that either you get out at the appointed time, or move onto another hourly or daily rate.

Alternatively, you can block book a studio in a 'lock out' arrangement. This means that you have 24 hour access to the studio, and you can leave all your equipment set up between sessions. A block booking will attract a special rate of course, but you have to bear in mind that time will be wasted while you and your musicians

Studio owner's view – Jerry Boys of Livingston Studios

(pic courtesy Brudce L Davies)

Jerry Boys is co-owner of Livingston Studio, a twin studio complex with SSL 48 track and Amek 24 track rooms, and is a widely respected engineer himself with credits including The Beatles, The Rolling Stones, Jimi Hendrix, Kate Bush and more recently Everything But The Girl, Lisa Stansfield and REM.

Choice of studio

'One factor is the type of record they are making. Is it a largely MIDI based record or is it a 'musician' based record? In the latter case they would need a decent recording room with proper acoustics and a good selection of microphones. For the former case they might need other technological type facilities. Most of the upmarket studios would try and cover both areas but their main rooms would be leaning towards 'musician' recording. Like ourselves they would all provide a basic computer, software, some sort of sync interface and a few sound modules. Some studios have a separate MIDI room as part of their facility.'

Rates

'In this day and age we try and be competitive. We are not among the cheapest but we offer excellent value for money. We operate in the lower third of the top echelon of studios, price wise. We range between £475 (plus VAT etc) per day in our smaller room and £650 in our bigger room.'

House engineers

'Our house engineers are important, and have become a more important feature in recent years. In the 80s it became the fashion not to use house engineers, but it has sort of come back in fashion. I guess it is because they are often cheaper, and they are often better because they know the studio and how it works, and how it sometimes doesn't work!'

The console

'The console would be a major factor in a producer's choice, whether he wants SSL or Neve, or something cheaper or different. We have an Amek room and people will choose that if they perhaps don't want to go SSL, but also if they are on a relatively tight budget. Most of the major manufacturers' consoles are OK in terms of sound these days. It's really down to ease of operation and whether they have the facilities you want. The top line consoles like Neve and SSL have sounds of their own, and they have automation systems that people are familiar with.'

Geography

'We find geography is important. People come to us because we are a long way from the record companies! (Livingston is in Wood Green, London, whereas most of the record companies are in the West End) They like to feel they are locked away a bit, from involvement with the A&R department shall we say. On other occasions where the A&R people are having a strong input, we may lose the gig because we are not close to the record company.'

Vibe

'I think the most difficult thing to quantify would be what we call vibe. I think that's the one thing where you can as a studio create your own unique space in the world. Most studios these days are built by competent acousticians and they have equipment from the same manufacturers. There is not a lot of difference apart from the mixing console and the colour scheme. What you can influence, and where you can carve out a particular character, is the vibe. We try to be very informal and yet efficient at the same time.'

Recreation

'We provide private lounges for both studios. There's a general entertainments area upstairs with a pool table, music, TV, satellite and all that sort of thing. If you have got a band in, a lot of people want to be able to sit somewhere outside of the control room. Wood Green is well endowed with all sorts of restaurants and takeaways: Chinese, Malayan, Greek,

Pizza Hut, MacDonalds. There are plenty within ten minutes walk, and many within half that distance. We provide a kitchen here and some people cook for themselves.'

Maintenance

'Maintenance is important in terms of keeping people happy while they are with you, and you hope then for return work. It is an area that is quite expensive and you have to be careful that you provide a proper level without spending too much money. We have a guy who comes in three times a week, and then he's on call the rest of the time. Then there's normally myself or another experienced engineer on site. A lot of faults are not really faults, they are operator errors. Most things in fact get sorted out by someone who's already here. On the odd occasion when we do get a major breakdown the maintenance engineer can be here within half an hour.'

Studio 2 at Livingston Studios (pic courtesy Brudce L Davies)

The control room of Studio 1 at Livingston Studios(pic courtesy Brudce L Davies)

are sleeping, or even taking days off over long periods of recording. Residential studios often operate on a lock out basis.

Negotiate the rate!

Studios won't like me saying this, but rates are often negotiable. It depends how much clout you have of course, but a major record company will expect to see a discount somewhere between modest and bailiff-inducing. Indeed, the reason why many studios have gone bust is because record companies have been playing off one studio against another to drive rates down.

Obviously, business is business and it comes down to survival of the fittest, but for what you get in a top studio in terms of equipment, acoustics and accommodation, the price you pay is often extraordinarily good value, if you consider what a decent studio costs to set up and run.

What you get for your money

The quoted rates would include standard equipment, analogue multitrack and an assistant engineer. If you need an experienced engineer, then expect to pay according to the depth of that experience (you know what you get when you pay peanuts!). Having the piano tuned will be extra, as may be the use of the studio's Hammond organ or other exotic equipment.

Studios normally prefer to supply tape rather than allowing clients to bring in their own. Obviously this is another profit centre for them, but it allows a degree of quality control, and certainty that the tape machines will be lined up correctly for that particular brand and type. If you do bring in your own tape, as you may if a project has been started elsewhere, then expect to pay the studio a handling charge to cover editing, leadering and labelling etc, as you would pay corkage if you took your own bottle of wine to a restaurant.

Overtime

If your session goes on until the early hours, then you will have to pay taxi costs for the studio's staff, and any telephone calls you make will be logged and charged to your session. Don't forget the VAT on top of all this. You may negotiate a discount for payment in advance, but if you don't, bear in mind that you probably won't be taking any tapes away until you have paid in full, not unless you are known to the studio anyway and have set up an account with them.

All of these extra costs may seem off-putting, but they are all part of the recording process, so just keep in mind how much money you are going to make at the end of it all. Unfortunately, many acts never make enough money to pay their recording costs back to the record company. It's a tough business, and nobody ever said it wasn't – take your chance and give it your best.

*I*n the studio, the recording process will vary according to the style of your music. As I mentioned when I covered pre-production, a guitar band may prepare in a rehearsal studio, or even on the road, but they will come into the studio with nothing actually recorded. A dance act on the other hand will probably have a significant amount of pre-programmed material which only needs to be dumped from the MIDI gear onto tape.

Those who rely solely on their sequenced MIDI systems right the way through to the mix are very much the exception. Tape, by the way, is still the preferred storage medium for most producers, but hard disk multitracks such as the Otari Radar are rapidly gaining in popularity. For the purpose of this article, I'll talk about recording a band with a drum kit, guitars and keyboards, but just about everything I shall say can be applied to other styles of music too.

Backing tracks

Any dictionary will tell you that a band is a group of musicians who play together. 'Together' is the operative word here because in a multitrack recording studio it is quite possible to record each instrument separately. If you do it this way however you will probably end up with a recording that has all the instruments playing all the right notes in all the right places, but it lacks that indefinable something that makes it sound like a band. It is usual therefore to record the basic instruments – drums, bass and rhythm guitar – all at the same time to get the feel of a real band playing together, and then add vocals, solo instruments and embellishments one by one as overdubs. The basic instruments form the so-called 'backing track' or 'basic tracks' – often referred to simply as 'the track'. 'Tracking' is the process of recording the backing tracks, although some people use the word to cover overdubs as well so that it means the entire recording process apart from the mixing.

The set up

Setting up to record the backing track takes some time, and it is common to finish recording all the backing tracks for an album before starting on the overdubs. Setting up the drum kit alone, with however many microphones the engineer chooses to use, could take the best part of a day depending on how picky you are going to be about the sound. As a producer, you obviously want to get a really good sound on the record, and a skilled engineer will be able to offer you a good drum sound in a couple of hours.

Setting up the other instruments and the mic for the guide vocal is straightforward in comparison, and you should be able to relax and collect your thoughts while the engineer and his or her assistant work on the mics and mixing console.

On the red light

When everything is ready, then one of the key moments in the production process has arrived. The band are going to lay down the backing track for what will hopefully be their next hit single. This has got to be right, and you are the person who has to make it so. Let the band play through the song a few times so that they can get used to the headphones and check foldback levels with the engineer. You will be thinking about the sound of each instrument, and each drum of the drum kit, from both technical and musical points of view. While realising that you are not hearing the final mix, you will be considering how the instruments blend, and whether the tempo is the same as it was in the rehearsal studio. You may need to discuss subtle musical points with one or more of the band. Maybe the bass player is dragging notes out when they would be better cut short. Perhaps the guitarist hasn't settled into this rhythm yet and will need a few more runs through. Maybe they are all just a little bit nervy because they don't have much studio experience and they have forgotten that if they make a mistake, the engineer can wind back the tape and they can try it again.

If you have a particular sound in mind that you want to achieve, then it may take some time experimenting with mics and mic positions to achieve precisely what you want. You are the producer, so you're in charge. Take as long as you like, but remember that you're responsible for sticking to the budget too!

How many takes?

As many as are necessary, of course. There is no point in going any further and overdubbing to a backing track which isn't absolutely right. This is where your skill as a producer comes in. Probably the most important part of your role is to know when something is right, and this isn't nearly as easy as it seems. Absolute perfection is unattainable, but many successful records are less than perfect technically, with wrong or missed notes and rhythmic inconsistencies. Yet despite this they sound great! The producer should be able to spot a great take, even when there could be some musical errors. If you have captured such a take and recognise its quality, you then have to decide whether to use it as it is, or try and fix the problems. You can fix the odd duff chord in a guitar track with punch ins, where the engineer jabs the record button just before the section that needs to be replaced and, by hitting the play or stop button, punches out afterwards.

Editing the backing track

If the band has lost the rhythm at one point, then this is a bigger problem. The same thing applies if a take has started really well and has then broken down. In both of these cases, the solution is to edit the multitrack master tape and use sections from two or more takes spliced together. The engineer will do this for you while you pace up and down in the corridor outside if need be. Taking a razor blade to two inch 24 track tape is not a task for the faint hearted since if it goes wrong, then you have lost all.

It hardly ever does go wrong however because the engineer will know from experience whether or not an edit will work. The main possibility why it might not work is if the tempo has changed from one take to another and there is a sudden gear shift. You can avoid this by getting the band to listen to a metronome ticking at the correct tempo before each take, or even getting them to play to a click track. This latter solution is rather drastic, and it is something that really needs to have been planned for from the rehearsal stage.

Creative editing

Some producers regard editing as a creative process in its own right and will actively seek out the best parts from all the takes the band has done. I asked at the beginning of this section how many takes are enough. Since I know you are dying to have a figure, let me say that some bands have as few as three takes in them, and if they don't get it within those three takes, then 33 wouldn't be enough and it's best to move onto a different song and have another go on another day. Other bands really can keep going, and once they know that they have one take in the can which is good enough, they will relax and keep getting better and better.

Overdubs

When the tension of recording the backing track is over, the overdubbing stage is where the creative ideas flow thick and fast. (In a MIDI-originated recording, I would probably say that when the tedium of dumping the backing tracks to tape is over...). Being creative is fun, fun, fun – as long as the ideas keep coming. It's when the ideas stop flowing that everyone turns to the producer. It's no good calling yourself the leader of the gang and then turning to someone else to ask, 'What shall we do now?'. Usually, overdubs get

Punch ins in a backing track can be noticeable where the spill from the other instruments suddenly disappears then comes back again, so listen carefully, and preferably have the engineer bounce the original take and the punch ins onto a new track for safety.

off to a good start and things seem to be going well. That's because you and the musicians are using up the stockpile of ideas that has been built up during pre-production and the early part of the recording process. There will come a point however when it is obvious that the recording needs something, but no-one knows quite what that something is. Often it is very difficult to be creative when you know the clock is ticking and you are effectively flushing £50 notes down the toilet.

There are strategies you can use to allow the collective creativity of you and the band to shine through. Here are a few ideas:

If you listen closely to successful records you will realise that they are often very simply constructed. Don't underestimate how difficult it is to achieve that simplicity.

- If you have recorded all the backing tracks for the album before starting on the overdubs, then you can skip backwards and forwards according to which song you most feel like working on. If you run out of ideas on one, change over to another one.
- Equip the band members with cheap cassette multitrackers (they probably have them already) and give them copies of the work in progress. Send them away to work on their ideas instead of hanging around the studio's pool table.
- Equip the band with multitrackers before any recording starts and let them work with copies of the rough demos. Tell them that you want as many musical ideas as you can get – the crazier the better. You can pick and choose later.
- Unless you think there might be a clash of egos, let the musicians swap instruments where possible. The guitarist might bash out a simple idea on the keyboard that the keyboard player himself might not have thought of.
- Encourage an attitude of being receptive to trying things out. It is common for people to jump on an idea and say that it won't work without giving it more than a few seconds consideration. This hardly encourages creativity. Have 'brainstorming' sessions where all you do is think of ideas, and no-one criticises them until later.

You may of course have the opposite problem, where there are too many ideas and you need to refine them down into something that is simple, but exactly right for the song. This is very much more difficult than it sounds, but if you listen closely to successful records you will realise that they are often very simply constructed. Don't underestimate how difficult it is to achieve that simplicity. A successful producer is someone who can encourage the generation of many ideas, and then discard the vast majority of them leaving only the ones that will blend together to create the perfect sound.

Recording vocals

And so the nightmare begins. Since the vocal is the most important component of the recording of any song, it has to be exactly right. But getting it exactly right is the most difficult part of the entire recording process. Singers come in three basic types: First there is the top class performer who always gets it right, and the only other possibility is that he or she might go for another take and sing even better. Among people who call themselves singers, this type is one in a thousand! Usually you will be working with the second type who is someone who obviously can sing, but under the studio spotlight many defects become significant. The third category of singer is someone who has been chosen for his or her looks or personality and sings like a donkey. You're in big trouble here, but you've got to pull through!

There are certain actions you can take to make sure the vocal is recorded as well as possible. Let's start with things that help even the best singers, and then work up to the more drastic solutions.

Improving the voice

We take it for granted that a champion tennis player needs a coach. So a top singer needs a coach too.

It isn't widely appreciated, but even the top singers need help to allow them to sing the way they do. There are two types of people who work with singers to improve their performance. One is a singing teacher who will help with the production of the sound, and the other is a voice coach who will help with the performance of a song. For our requirements, a basic singing teacher is probably the best option. (Bear in mind that some people who advertise themselves as 'voice coaches' work with speech rather than singing, so be careful not to get confused).

Most singing teachers specialise in musicals or classical singing rather than pop, rock or Death Metal, but the principles of voice training are very similar. Anyone with a weak, wobbly voice, lacking in range will benefit enormously from two or three months of weekly lessons.

Even if the teacher doesn't understand the style of music in which you are working and thinks your singer wants to be the Phantom of the Opera, it will still work. It's like going to the gym – you do exercises in there that bear no relation to any activity you would perform in real life, but if you go regularly you will end up feeling fit and looking good. Go to singing lessons and your voice will feel fit and it will sound good, in any style of music.

Singing teacher's view – Helena Shenel

People whom Helena Shenel has helped with their singing include Paul Young, Annie Lennox, Peter Gabriel and George Michael.

Using the voice correctly

'I don't teach people a style, I teach people how to use the voice and the muscles involved in singing correctly so that they don't strain anything and get the best possible development out of their particular voice.'

Screaming heavy metal singers too?

'They are all using the same instrument. I show them how to use it without damaging it.'

Why do top singers go to her?

'To make sure that they do nothing to strain the voice. They might be going on tour or have a heavy recording schedule, and they would ask me ways of strengthening the voice and making sure that it doesn't get tired.'

Singing out of tune

'That's a bit difficult. A student of mine first came to me saying that he really really wanted to sing, but I had to ask him if he realised that he couldn't sing in tune. Added to that he made a noise which was akin to something between a bull bellowing and a donkey braying – painful. We persevered for about three years and he eventually became a very good singer. It is amazing what you can do with someone who really wants to do it, but you need patience. Sometimes

people can't sing in tune because they are pushing and forcing the voice beyond what nature intended it to do. One of my most important things is that you can't pronounce words the same way as you would speak them because you run the risk of singing out of tune.'

Breathing

'Breathing should be as natural as possible. I never give people special breathing exercises. I teach them how to sing not how to breathe. You can breathe very well and be a long distance swimmer, it doesn't necessarily mean that you can sing well.'

How many lessons?

'It depends so much on the individual. A young man singing with a band came to me for an hour long consultation. I told him about putting his head and neck in the right position, opening his mouth correctly and all the various things. At the end of the lesson he said 'I can't believe it, it's absolutely amazing the difference it makes'. A few days later after a gig he told me that his voice felt so much stronger, it didn't get tired or hoarse and the band all thought he sounded better. That was after one lesson. It depends to a large extent on whether the person has an open mind and is willing to accept my ideas. I do occasionally get a bit of resistance if people are unwillingly sent by their managers or record companies, but generally I find that people with the most outrageous public personae are really very nice people with a very good professional attitude.'

Warm up!

Once you have taken steps to make sure that the singer's voice is at the peak of condition, then it is up to you to decide how to handle the session. It isn't as commonly known as it should be that even a good singer needs a lengthy warm up session before he or she can sing at peak performance. It is normal for this warm up to take as long as an hour before the voice achieves real depth and fullness of sound – start recording too soon and you will have to use effects units to strengthen the voice artificially. Of course it is important not to overstretch the voice during the warm up and wear it out so watch out for any sign that the singer is straining.

Experienced vocalists will have their own warm up routine, which they will probably want to carry out in private, so you should arrange a space where they can be on their own. An inexperienced singer, or one who has not yet recognised the need for a warm up, will need a certain amount of coaxing. Get them to sing other songs in their repertoire to loosen up. Once the voice is fully fit, or perhaps a little earlier, you can start rehearsing the song.

Once again, many singers don't understand the need for rehearsal and would probably just dive straight into recording. It's not your song, (probably) so don't go telling them how they should sing it, but listen to what they are doing and seek out ways in which whatever there is inside the singer can be brought out to the maximum. Probably the most important factor is the phrasing of each line, how it starts and ends, how much weight is given to each word and to each note. Working on phrasing will need skills that can only be developed with experience – but eventually you will be able to take a raw performance and double its effectiveness.

Of course you should also consider details like intonation, and whether the words are intelligible. If a particular note seems to be a problem, see if you can get the singer to recognise and correct the problem before recording commences.

Match the mic to the voice

With the help of the engineer you will select a microphone that works well with the singer's voice, and sort out other technical matters. Many producers these days record a number of takes of the vocal, maybe as many as six or eight, and then sort through them later to get the best version of each line. With a little bit of skill you and the engineer will be able to compile the best of all of these versions, perhaps to the extent of swapping between takes on every line, or even the odd word where necessary. After this, there may still be the odd line that doesn't sound quite right, so you'll have to get the vocalist back in again to correct it. You may worry that since the time required to compile several takes into one can be quite lengthy, the vocalist may come back with a different tone of voice. Indeed, this may be a problem, but it is better than leaving a line in an unusable state.

If you listen very carefully to records made by people chosen by the record company for their looks or personality, you will almost certainly be able to hear these inconsistencies. If it were possible to

If you can't make out some of the words without close scrutiny of the lyric sheet (which you should have a copy of), then consider whether the song could be improved with a little extra clarity in the vocal delivery. Sometimes the opposite is preferable!

Producer's view – Gary Langan

Gary Langan is a well respected engineer/producer, with credits including Paul McCartney, Public Image, Scritti Politti, Hothouse Flowers, Spandau Ballet and The Art of Noise.

Recording the band together

'If I was recording a band, I would like to have all the band playing in the studio and the vocalist singing. Without a vocalist you don't have anything. Then I'll work on that and see what, if anything, needs rearranging or repairing. If I am working with a band it is very important that I have all the information there all the time. Also, a musician in a band is getting off on what his mates are doing. You can't really get off on sitting in a bloody great room with a pair of headphones strapped to your head looking at nobody. To me, that just cannot be fun, and if you are not having fun and you're not enjoying yourself, then you are not going to give me the ultimate performance, which is what I need. I can get around every other problem but there is no substitute for the ultimate performance.'

The guide vocal

'If the performance is good enough and it is recorded well enough, then there is no reason why it can't stay. It may be that just bits of it may stay. I'll certainly hang onto it until the end. I won't erase it because there may be something that occurred while that was going on that might be useful when we come back later to redo the vocals. Even though the guide vocal might not be perfectly in tune or in time, maybe the sense of what the singer was trying to put across was right, so I can always go back and show him what he was giving as a performance when everyone was playing together.'

How many takes of the basic tracks?

'I don't have a problem with putting a razor blade through the tape. On average I'll do somewhere around three or four takes and I'll edit from that. I much prefer to use an analogue machine and I enjoy editing tape. I recently recorded a track in four takes and portions of all four takes went to make the master. '

Matching tempi between takes

'I listen to the bits I am going to put together. Maybe I would preview what I was thinking of doing on the multitrack on quarter inch if I was uncertain. If the band is OK at playing to a click track then you wouldn't have tempo changes, but I wouldn't force them to play to a click. That's like making someone who is left handed write with their right hand.'

record a perfect vocal in one take, everyone would do it that way. Unfortunately the singers who are capable of doing this are, as I said, very few and far between.

As a last resort – cheat!

If the worst comes to the worst and you just can't get a satisfactory recording, then you will have to use a little studio trickery – or a lot of it if necessary. This can range from, double tracking, pitch shifting

Producer's View – Ian Curnow

Keyboard player and programmer Ian Curnow, together with his engineer partner Phil Harding, came through the Stock, Aitken and Waterman PWL 'Hit Factory' and now have their own studio at The Strongroom which allows them to offer a complete production package to record companies.

On working with the band

'I know musicians who can play fantastic things that can just blow me away, but whether it's right for the record is another thing. It's part of the producer's job to limit players of awesome technical ability to just doing the right thing! Especially drummers.'

Problem singers

'Many of the people we work with have problems. Since our PWL days of manufacturing records, as people have accused us of doing, we have got used to working with people who can't actually sing very well. For the last two years we have made full use of Steinberg's Time Bandit with Cubase Audio. Quite often we will only push a singer until we have what we feel is a good performance, knowing that we can retime and retune it later. You can correct tuning, timing and volume with technology. The one thing you can't get from technology is the performance. If the performance is there and the singer is delivering a message to the listener, we can make it palatable by putting it in tune. It's nice if they can sing it in tune, but once you recognise that you are not going to get that, it's a question of going for lots of takes and getting as much of a performance as possible.'

The vocal session

'Both of us will sit there during a vocal session. Phil will push the singer to the limit of their performance, while I will consider whether I can retime or retune it. We try and record a vocal quite quickly these days. If we have a performance there in two hours, we'll leave it and and work on it later for six or eight hours. We usually record the vocal in chunks. We'll record the chorus and then tackle the first verse. Anything that is going to be repeated, we will only record once and use that performance each time.'

out of tune notes using a Harmonizer, or sampling a line and tweaking the pitch bend control as you record it back to tape, to a total reconstruction of the vocal using an audio sequencer with time and pitch correction software. If you think this is extreme, then let me assure you that it is in fact normal to do anything that is necessary to achieve a perfect vocal, because that is what is going to sell the song. If you don't have the technical skills yourself to take on these tasks, sit back and let the engineer or programmer do it for you. All you have to do is decide when it's right!

*Just a small section of Phil Harding and Ian
Curnow's well equipped studio*

*M*uch has been written about mixing from an engineer's point of view, not so much from a producer's point of view however. Many years ago, before the modern era of multitrack, recording and mixing were part of the same process. You had to get a good balance between the voices and instruments at the session because there was no way of making any adjustments later. In fact much orchestral music is recorded in the same way today, directly to stereo. Mixing directly to stereo is also very common for today's popular music, in live PA work and broadcasting.

Why multitrack?

The reason that it is possible to do without a multitrack stage in these situations is that the engineer knows before even one fader has been lifted what the final recording should sound like – as close to the original as possible. Since skilled engineers can achieve such remarkable results, you might wonder why we need a multitrack stage at all. The answer is that it allows much more attention to be paid to each element of the recording in terms of sound quality, musicality and creativity. Paying as much attention to these three aspects as they deserve is why recording takes so long and why you have to put so much effort into it.

The producer should ideally start the mixing process as soon as the project gets off the ground. He should have an idea of the sound he is aiming for, allowing a certain amount of scope for creativity depending on the nature of the project – the requirement for creativity sometimes being great, sometimes comparatively modest. If it is a dance music record, for instance, then the producer will understand the style well enough to know the elements of the music that his audience demand, and will add to those elements new and different sounds and textures to push the style further into the future.

If the producer knows how every step of the preparation and recording process is going to contribute to the final mix, then the mixing stage should be straightforward and successful. This means, among other things, getting the arrangement right and selecting the right sounds, making sure the musicians are playing in time and in tune, obtaining a good performance from the singer by whatever means necessary. If there is a problem in any of these areas, then you can only turn a deaf ear to it for so long – until the mix in fact.

Any problems present on the tape at the mixing stage will have to be disguised or covered up. Those problems should have been corrected as soon as they occurred.

Monitor mix

As more and more tracks are being added to the recording during the overdubbing stage, then the engineer and producer will be working with a mix that may bear a passing resemblance to the finished product – the monitor mix. The monitor mix is what you listen to during the recording process, and is usually thought of as a rough guide to what is already on the tape. Good enough so that the musicians can get a proper feel for the music, and good enough to tell the producer how the recording is shaping up.

Monitor mix facilities
It depends on the type of mixing console you are using, but some have only very basic monitor facilities – perhaps just level, pan and a couple of auxiliary sends. This means that you can't do anything in the monitor mix apart from set how loud each instrument is, where it appears in the stereo image, and how much reverb it has (the other aux will be used to send foldback to the musicians' headphones). In fact this is not a bad way of working because you will hear exactly what is on the tape as you progress through the recording. Hopefully you will be perfecting each sound as it is created, and you will add new sounds in context with what is already there. If the monitor mix sounds good, then you can be sure the final mix will sound great.

This simple style of monitor mixing has its merits, but large scale consoles offer vastly more sophisticated monitoring facilities. You can create a mix on the monitors using EQ, compression, gating and everything else that is part of modern studio technique. If you regard the monitor mix as something temporary, but you – and the engineer – then proceed to use all of these facilities, you may find yourself in big trouble by the time you flip the multitrack onto the big faders and start to mix from flat because the sound will be totally different. But you wouldn't do that of course.

The first rule of recording
By the time you graduate to SSL or AMS-Neve class studios, you will have learnt the first rule of recording: Nothing less than 100% effort

is good enough. You should regard everything you do as being part of the finished product and make it as perfect as possible. Even if it is only something you do as an experiment or as a temporary reference, then the fact that you have done it right will at least tell you something if it didn't work quite as well as you had hoped, and what you have tried and discarded will still influence the mix. This includes the monitor mix.

With a console that has only rudimentary monitoring facilities you will tend to want to perfect everything on tape. With a console that has sophisticated monitoring facilities, you will record a good clean sound on tape, and then anything that you do to the monitor mix will become part of the final mix. The console will allow you to do this so you don't have to start from scratch when the overdubs are finished. In fact you can do this with any console that has enough channels.

It is very common once a few tracks have been recorded to route the multitrack to the channel faders and start to mix as overdubs progress. This way you never get to a point when you say, 'Right that's finished, let's clear the desk and start to mix'. You just come to a realisation that everything is done and all that is needed is a little polishing here and there.

Self-produced artist George Michael works in this way and his regular appearances at the top of the sales charts confirm the value of this philosophy.

From another point of view

There are many ways to make a record, and I can imagine some producers reading the above and thinking what a load of bull it is. There is another style of recording where the approach to an album is to record all the basic tracks, then to overdub all the other instruments and vocals, then to take a few days break before starting to mix the whole lot. The disadvantage of working a song at a time all the way from basic tracks to mix is that you can easily lose perspective.

People on average listen to each record they buy about six times before they store it in a cardboard box in the attic, give it to an unloved relative or donate it to a charity jumble sale. The producer of the record has to listen to it something more like 600 times – or more – during the recording and mixing process, and in the same way as familiarity breeds contempt, over-familiarity with a song and the recording of that song means that you can't judge it in the same way as a punter would.

> Nothing less than 100% effort is good enough. You should regard everything you do as being part of the finished product and make it as perfect as possible.

Engineer's view – Paul Gomersall

Paul Gomersall has enjoyed the privilege of engineering George Michael's 'comeback' album *Older* where George, as usual, was his own producer. Other credits include work with producers Trevor Horn, Phil Collins (Collins working as a producer), Stephen Hague, Stephen Lipson, Thomas Dolby, Chris Porter, Laurie Latham and others.

Working with producers who are engineers themselves

'Producers like to distance themselves from the desk, as long as they have an engineer they can trust. It's one of the joys of production. If they have a problem then they might dive in and try and sort it out themselves, but usually there won't be a problem. You are the interface with all the technical stuff so the producer doesn't have to think about that. If the producer comes up with an idea you make it work for them. With computers, recording is becoming more and more technical.'

What should an engineer do if a producer appears not to hear a problem?

'Point it out. One of the good phrases is, 'I think we should listen back to that', He will be listening by then. There are ways of getting your point across. Diplomacy is a big part of the job.'

Working with George Michael

Monitoring

'I give him the mix output of the desk in his headphones. The headphone mix is very important to anyone. That's what they are listening to in the studio so that's what they want to hear in the headphones. If someone wants to hear a little bit more of the snare, you just push it up.'

Reverb

'The way he sings the consonants it gives a bit of excitement to his vocal sound. It's being used as another instrument. I generally set up two, three or four reverbs that I think will suit the track as it's coming together and take it from there and George will pick what he wants.'

Mixing with George

'The mix is an evolutionary thing. We start a song and virtually every song we do we work through to the mix. You never get a stage where everything is finished and you start mixing. It evolves and somewhere along the line he'll want to do a vocal ride so we'll switch the mix computer on, then we'll switch it off again and add some more things and continue like that. I know when we are finished when he says let's put one down. He'll take a mix home and come back the next day and probably continue working on it. The programming diminishes as the work carries on and we get more involved in riding levels of things and EQ and other bits and pieces. And then suddenly it's there. It's finished. The rough mixes are really important because sometimes he will ask to refer to something we had done before and then carry on from there. So we keep all the mixes we have done in case one of them had something that was really good.'

Take a break

Taking a break between recording and mixing means that you can come back to the song with a fresh pair of ears and hear very clearly which are the good bits that need to be brought out, and which elements play an important but subservient role. If this is the philosophy of mixing that appeals to you more strongly, then you should be aware that it would probably be a waste of time working on an elaborate monitor mix. You could store it on a console with recall facilities, but that would negate the advantages of taking a break before mixing. A simple monitor mix is probably the best idea.

Still on the subject of monitor mixes, another common thing to do is to swap between songs during overdubbing according to which one you and the band feel you have most enthusiasm for at the moment. Or you may have booked a session player who you want on more than one song, so he might as well do them all in the same session. This means locating to each song on the multitrack and resetting the monitor mix on the console. If you confine yourself to level/pan/reverb monitor mixes then it won't take too long to set up.

Sometimes however, during the later stages of overdubbing, you may feel that the mix you are hearing sounds really great, just by chance, and you would like to keep it as a reference for when you start mixing proper. In this case it's a simple matter to copy the monitor mix onto a DAT so you can check it later. With so few variable elements, it is pretty easy for a skilled engineer to reconstruct the mix almost exactly, and then you can go ahead and improve it still further.

How do I get a good mix?

Simple. Use a good engineer and stay clear! I mentioned earlier in the series that engineers acquire a vast amount of experience of working with music and sound, and they are the people who should be operating the faders – not the producer, unless the producer comes from an engineering background of course.

If the producer sits in the studio from the moment the first fader is raised all the way through to the finish, he will be nothing but an inhibition for the engineer who would really like to get on and tinker with the sounds and try out lots of ideas, many of which might not work. So this will be a good time for you to take a walk in the fresh air and clear your mind ready to make an objective judgment on how the mix is progressing, two or three hours after you left the engineer alone with it.

You may leave behind a few ideas or guidelines, or you may even encourage the engineer to go wild and try out some crazy things. When you return, you will hear your production in all its glory and you will be able to advise on what it is you want more of, what you want less of, or you could even say that it is entirely wrong and you want to start again. An experienced engineer accepts that the producer is in charge and won't take offence (he just won't work with you again!).

What is a good mix?

A trickier question is what makes a good mix. It's especially tricky for the engineer who has to learn every detail of how to get a good mix, since nothing will happen by its own accord. A producer on the other hand doesn't need to know the details but has to be able to recognise when something is right, and offer meaningful comments when it isn't.

You need to keep in mind the purpose of the mix. Is it a dance floor mix that should sound great on a club PA? Or is it intended for CD listening at home? A radio mix should emphasise the 'buy me' factor, whatever it is that will attract the listener to the singles counter of the record store. The engineer will always sit in the optimum listening position directly between the speakers while mixing, but you will probably wander around the room. This is so you have the opportunity to hear the mix in less than perfect conditions, which is exactly the way the end user will hear it. Either they will be in a club with the bass turned up to stomach pounding volume, or they have a rubbishy home hifi with the speakers wired out of phase, or they are listening on a car radio in heavy traffic, with a hole in the exhaust.

Your mix has to sell the song in each of these situations so while the engineer considers the finer points which will only be appreciated by those with good quality home stereo systems or a decent pair of headphones, you will be looking for the overall impact. If the mix sounds good from any listening position in the control room, then it probably is good. All studios have two or more pairs of monitors so you can check the mix on very high quality speakers or on the console-mounted near fields. You can also have a cassette copy made so you can check the mix on a cheap stereo system, on a Walkman or in the car. The more ways you can listen to the mix the better.

Stereo format

As you know, most multitrack recordings are mixed to DAT these days, but at a professional level, DAT isn't always considered to be

The Rapino Brothers in their studio with Kylie Minogue

entirely satisfactory. For one thing it is only 16 bit, which means that its sound quality isn't any better than the CD people will listen to at home. The engineer therefore has absolutely no headroom to play with, and inevitably there is a margin of unused capability that makes the recording not quite as good technically as it ought to be. It won't be too long before we see 20 or even 24 bit stereo formats in the studio on a regular basis, although it might be some years before any one is accepted as a standard.

In the meantime, many producers are opting for the 'old fashioned' alternative of analogue reel to reel tape. They don't used a battered old Revox however. Top studios will have a slightly worn but well maintained Ampex or Studer stereo machine that runs at a speed of 30 inches per second (twice the speed of 15 ips, long considered the professional norm) and takes half inch rather than quarter inch tape. Such a machine isn't totally transparent but has a definite sound of its own, and it's a sound that producers like, particularly if a recording has been made on a digital rather than analogue multitrack. The frequency response is in fact better than DAT or CD which can only manage around 20 kHz at the top end. Half inch analogue at 30 ips can go up to 25 kHz and beyond, and quiet signals can still be clearly heard below the already low noise floor – even without Dolby SR noise reduction.

There are many who will say that half inch is better than digital for these reasons, and so many successful records have been mixed to half inch that it is very difficult to disagree.

When the stereo master is finished, then the producer's work still

Remixer's view – Marco Sabiu of the Rapino Brothers

The Rapino Brothers are Marco Sabiu and Charlie Mallozzi. (They are not real brothers obviously – 'rapino' is Italian for robber). They have built up a significant and lucrative following among record companies making new versions of original recordings by Take That, Roxette, Sleeper, Suggs, Rozalla, Dubstar among many others.

The need for remixing
'I'm not the one who said remixing was necessary. It's the record companies who want remixes because they want to have their songs played in the clubs. If people like the song in the clubs then they will go and buy the record.'

On following record company's instructions
'Sometimes they tell us what kind of style they want. Sometimes they don't tell us anything, they just give us the vocal and we just do what we want. Usually we only keep the vocals and we redo everything, unless it's a band with guitars then maybe we'll keep the riff. It depends. It can be almost like doing a new song.'

Remixers versus the original producer
'I listen to the original producer's mix to try to get the kind of vibe that they used so I can avoid doing the same thing. I don't know whether producers like what we do. We always do a radio version of a remix and sometimes the record company will use it as a single. If that version goes into the charts I think the producer should be quite happy because the album will sell better.'

Remixing as a way of getting into production
'I can't see any difference between a remix and a production because at the end of the day when you do a remix you start from scratch. The only thing you have is the vocal. To me that is a production.'

Technical knowledge
'On that side we are quite lucky because when I was in Italy I worked as a sound engineer, so for me now it's helpful to have that kind of knowledge. If I want a sound I know how to do it. I don't have to ask someone else which would be just wasting time. I think it's quicker and better if you have a good knowledge of the machines you have. We have a Pro Tools system with Logic Audio so we do everything like that.'

Acoustic instruments
'We quite like to use live drums and real guitar and bass. When we do that we usually go into a bigger studio because we don't have the space. Then we come back to our place and transfer everything into the Pro Tools and we start editing.'

continues into the CD mastering studio. This is the very final stage where the stereo master is committed to a U-Matic video tape or Exabyte data cartridge. After this, no further alterations can be made to the sound. CD mastering isn't quite such a creative opportunity as vinyl mastering used to be (mostly because of the technical limitations of the vinyl medium), and still is on occasion. It is however a chance to make sure that all the tracks have the right relative levels, EQing and compressing where necessary. You will also set the length of the gaps between tracks, and perform any crossfades between tracks that you think are appropriate (and to hell with radio plays!).

When you leave the CD mastering studio your work as producer is complete and you can look forward to the financial rewards for your labours. Actually, you may also have to look forward to your recording being handed over to specialist remixers – a fact of life that you will accept as gracefully as a true professional would!

8 The business of music

*T*hink of the music business as a spider's web. All around are dotted the carcasses of unwary flies, some formerly fat and juicy, others so small that they were eaten up and spat out in an instant. The flies in my metaphorical web are musicians, songwriters, arrangers, producers, managers, A&R people, record company executives, music publishers, record, cassette and CD manufacturers, pluggers and marketers, DJs, radio stations, record shops, royalty collection agencies and others. That pretty well covers the whole of the music industry (except the music journalists who are far too agile ever to get trapped!).

So what kind of beast is it that sits at the centre of the web, growing fat at the expense of all the other poor creatures who have no option but to succumb to his deadly embrace? The music business lawyer of course!

Why use a lawyer?

You may have realised this already, but nothing happens in the music business without a lawyer being the go-between in the transaction. A few enlightened souls have discovered that it really is possible to do business on a handshake between honourable people, but for the vast majority, the only way is the legalistic way.

A record producer will definitely need to have a music business lawyer to examine his contract with a record company. The consequences of not doing so could be dire, from a potential loss of all royalties (royalties are often known as 'points' in the business, points being a percentage of sales revenue) through to responsibility for budget overruns and possibly even worse. The emphasis here has to be on a getting advice from a specialist music business lawyer.

Know the tricks

In the past, record companies have dreamed up all kinds of schemes for protecting their own interests against the interests of the creative people who actually earn the money. Although there seems to be a much more responsible attitude developing in the record companies these days, all the old clauses are pre-loaded into their word processors ready to be dropped into a contract.

One old favourite trick is known as cross collateralisation. This typically would allow a record company to offset profits earned on one album against losses made on another. Suppose as a producer you made two albums with a band. The first sold well but the other bombed. If cross collateralisation is allowed there will be no overall profit so your points will add up to zero. If your contract however specifically disallows cross collateralisation, as it should, then you will receive all the royalties you are entitled to on the first album while receiving nothing for the second (because you didn't do your job properly, did you?).

The funniest thing is that, despite my opening paragraph, the lawyers aren't the bad guys – it's all the people who have tried to screw each other (financially I mean) throughout the entire history of the music business since year zero. Despite many people's current best intentions, this tradition of distrust means that almost every word has to be inscribed on parchment, signed and sealed, and whether a project should succeed or fail, the lawyer always benefits.

Where does the money come from?

Money, in the music industry, is made from the exploitation of copyrights. 'Exploit' in this context is a good word, it means that your work is being promoted well and it is generating revenues. There are three basic types of copyright involved here. In a musical work of any kind there is a performing right and a mechanical right. and there is an additional copyright in a recording of that work.

Performing, mechanical and recording rights

The performing right means that the owner of the copyright can allow performances, whether live or recorded, of the music to take place in return for a fee. The mechanical right means that the owner of the copyright can allow the music to be recorded, and allow copies of that recording to be made and sold, once again for a fee.

It is important that you understand these methods of generating income because your livelihood will be very closely linked to them.

The third copyright is one that exists in the actual recording of the music rather than the music itself, and once again, owners of this copyright can allow the recording to be performed or broadcast in return for a fee. There are other copyrights involved in music, such as a musician's right in his or her own performance, but we'll stick to basics.

As a producer, you will not be entitled to any of these copyrights. The performing and mechanical rights will belong to the writer or his publisher, the rights in the recording will belong to the record company. (Of course, if you helped to write a song, then you will be entitled to a share of the performing and mechanical royalties).

At the moment it is virtually certain that your income as a producer will come from a combination of a flat fee combined with points. (Some producers, particularly remixers, only get a fee with no points.) The points will be a percentage of actual sales of records, cassettes and CDs. The more the record company sells, the more you will earn. If you consider that a top producer may be on something like three points, and a top act can sell millions of copies worldwide, you can estimate for yourself how much you are going to make when your production career really takes off!

The only snag with this arrangement is that sales are only one way in which recordings can be exploited. Performance royalties are a major component of any songwriter's or composer's income, in some cases making mechanicals look meagre in comparison. But do producers get points on performances of their work? They do not.

This is a major issue in the music world since, despite a recent upturn in sales, many people think that performance royalties are going to become the number one income generator for the entire record industry. Although you may be very keen to buy the latest CD by your favourite act right now, how will you feel about going to the trouble of buying a physical object when you can have the music delivered to you directly via the information superhighway at the cost of maybe a few pence a play?

Actually, that's still very much a debatable point, but producers certainly do have to debate it now rather than wait until their sales have declined into oblivion before they do anything about it.

Cover versions

The other side of the copyright coin is of relevance to producers of artists who do cover versions of other people's songs, and to producers who use samples from other recordings in their work. It used to be the case that once a song had been recorded, then anyone could make their own recording of it as long as the statutory royalty rate was paid.

This no longer applies and if you want to cover a song, you must apply to the copyright holder for permission. This permission is almost certain to be granted since cover versions are how songwriters and publishers make much of their income, but it would be unwise to record the song first and assume that permission would be forthcoming.

Using samples

In the case of samples, it has been common in the past simply to use samples and hope to get away with it. Once again this is unwise. (One major artist recently used a sample on an album without

If you think that any of the lyrics of a song need to be altered, to change the song from a male version to a female version for example, then you must be very careful to get permission to do this.

getting permission. Hundreds of thousands of copies had to be withdrawn from sale, the song re-recorded and the CD repressed, because of this one expensive mistake). The only exception to this is where a CD or CD-ROM is specifically produced for sampling purposes where once you have bought the product you are entitled to virtually unrestricted use.

Management

- You may be a brilliant musician, writer, engineer or producer, but are you a brilliant self publicist too, able to charm your way into A&R departments and get to work with the top acts?
- Can you be bothered to attend lengthy meetings with your lawyer making sure that every last comma in the contract with the record company is the place most favourable to your interests?
- Do you want to break off work every time the phone rings in case it's someone really important that you have to talk to?
- Do you think you could check a record company's books to make sure that your points have been correctly calculated and that funds haven't been siphoned off in a manner not allowed by your contract?
- Do you think it is worth paying 20% of your income to make sure all these things are properly and professionally handled, leaving you free to get on and produce?

Any sensible person will recognise the correct answer to the first four questions. The answer to the fifth is yes, because even though giving up 20% of your hard earned production fees and points seems like a high percentage, at least it's a percentage of something. Without a good manager you may be able to console yourself that you are keeping 100% of your income for yourself, but it may just be 100% of no income at all! Your manager may even, through his music business aware accountant, be able to recoup much of that 20% by making savings on your tax bill!

To get to be a record producer, you are going to have to be able to promote yourself in the early stages before you have established a track record of any kind. You won't find it difficult to find a band to produce, or a singer to work with, because natural-born producers have the ability to get on well with musicians and they are the kind of people that musicians instinctively trust.

If you don't think you are the kind of person that can get on well with musicians, you are going to find it difficult to become a record producer – although domineering, autocratic producers are not entirely unknown in the industry!

Selling yourself to a record company isn't going to be quite so easy, but if you are doing good work, then the opportunities are there. Once you have produced a few records that have sold reasonably well, then you are in a position to approach a manager.

What your manager will do

Once you have made an agreement with a manager, whether it is a handshake deal or a formal contract, the manager will make sure that A&R departments are aware of you and the type of music you work with. Your manager will keep his finger on the pulse of the business far more firmly than you would have time to do, and he'll know which acts are planning new recording projects, and whether they are shopping around for a new producer.

Record company negotiations

If an A&R manager becomes interested in you, then he will enter into a lengthy three way discussion between himself, your manager and the artist's manager. You will be relieved of all the nit-picking business details so that you only have to discuss the strictly musical aspects of the forthcoming recording.

If the record company thinks you are the right man or woman for the job, then your manager will negotiate your remuneration. Your manager will have a good idea of your current market value, and of how much the record company is likely to be willing to pay. You will get a better deal by going through a manager simply because he knows the business. If you think you might consider doing the negotiating yourself, pause for a moment to imagine how good a record producer the manager would be!

Working on the project

When the project gets under way, you will need to devote your entire attention to it during virtually all of your waking hours for a period of possibly two months or more for an album. Without a manager, how would you find time to line up your next job? It just isn't possible. Everyone in the industry has their own schedule – the record company has a certain number of releases to make, certain types of music sell better according to the time of year, the band has touring commitments and you have booked two weeks in Bognor in the middle of August! Juggling all of these is a full time occupation – your manager will let you get on and produce great music, which is probably all you ever wanted to do.

Collecting your share

When the recording is finished, in the shops and at the top of the charts, you will be able to sit back and count the money flowing in. Or will you? Collection agencies like the Performing Right Society, the Mechanical Copyright Protection Society and Phonographic Performance Limited look after virtually everyone's interest – apart from the producer.

The producer is paid according to what is received by the record company, after whatever deductions are specified in the contract. No reputable record company would intentionally pay a producer even a penny less than he was entitled to in the contract (although they might haggle over even these tiny amounts during the negotiation), but the complexity of the music retail industry means that opportunities for making large accounting errors exist in abundance.

Manager's view – Stephen Budd

Stephen Budd is a manager specialising in producers, engineers and remixers. His roster features Mike Hedges, Gus Dudgeon, Martyn Ware, the Rapino Brothers and many others. Their collective credits are far too many to mention!

Why a producer needs a manager

'Producers are not necessarily the best people to go after gigs themselves. They tend to be a little shy about pushing themselves forward. On a marketing level, there needs to be someone on the ground who can go and find out who's doing what and where, which bands have signed to which labels, which bands are hot, which bands are not. Then I try to market that producer to A&R people or artist managers so that their name is on the top of the pile. 'Reason number two is that producers find it difficult to negotiate deals. It's very difficult to have someone estimating your own value – it's a very personal issue. Producers are not always as clued in as they could be as to what their value is in the marketplace.

Sometimes they overvalue themselves. More often than not they undervalue themselves. My job is to create maximum income for producers, playing a delicate role without undermining them or losing the gig for the sake of it.

'The third thing is that a good producer should be working a lot of the time. If they are not, and they are good, they are probably not being represented properly. If they are in the studio all the time, the last thing they want to do is answer the phone every ten minutes to sort out scheduling and budgeting for the next project. Scheduling for somebody like Mike Hedges who has just had a massive hit record is horrendous. Every five minutes someone comes on the line with a great act that you would love to work with. It's very difficult to say no, but you're having to juggle with so many different elements: artist's time, producer's time, studio availability, engineer's time, the next artist the producer is going to work with.

'Lastly, somebody needs to be there to liaise on the money front, working out how much the record company can afford, setting a budget that works for both parties and making sure the record comes in on budget. That is a job that requires diplomatic skills. All of these elements come into play: marketing, negotiation and project management, these are the key reasons why a producer needs a manager.'

Any music business contract should include a clause stating that an independent accountant can be appointed to inspect the record company's relevant books and paperwork to make absolutely sure that no errors are made. This keeps the record company on their toes to make sure that every last penny goes to its intended recipient.

RePro – the Guild of Recording Producers, Directors and Engineers

RePro has grown out of The British Record Producers Guild which was established to give producers a unified voice in the music and recording industries. Current full members include Gus Dudgeon, Steve Lipson, Steve Levine, Rupert Hine, Chris Kimsey, Gary Langan, Hugh Padgham, Phil Wainman, Muff Winwood and Alan Winstanley. The President of RePro is George Martin and the Chairman is Robin Millar.

RePro's View, courtesy of Vice Chairman, Peter Filleul

RePro Activities

'RePro is a trade association which represents the profession of recording producers, sound directors and engineers. We provide them with a quarterly newsletter and usually about five forum meetings a year. We produce an annual A&R guide, a budget guide, and we are about to provide a legal guide which will advise them about producer contracts. We have three hotlines to professionals who provide free advice, usually up to about an hour's worth, ranging from legal advice to accounting and financial advice. We can provide various discounts on equipment which are very useful for people starting up. And of course we provide representation of the profession within bodies that are discussing the development of the music industry.

Also, our members become associate members of APRS (Association of Professional Recording Services) so they can attend meetings arranged by the APRS, which are usually more technically biased.'

Membership

'There are two main categories of membership: Full Membership and Associate Membership. Full Members must be recommended by other Full Members and would probably be those who have been around in the industry for a while and have a CV. We would stop people becoming Full Members if they were only part time producers for example. But if you are involved in the industry at almost any level, straight out of college even, or if you are going in as a tape op, you can become an Associate Member. We believe it is important for people starting off in the industry to have access to those who have been in it longer.

Then there are Overseas Associate memberships, which have exactly the same benefits as Associate membership except that you can't become a Full Member of RePro.

There is another special category of APRS Engineer membership for engineers who work for APRS studios. Freelance engineers can join as Associate Members. The only real differences between the categories is that Full Members have a vote and are entitled to take part in certain events, such as when a prestigious console manufacturer wants to talk to people who are likely to be working on an SSL or (AMS-Neve) Capricorn rather than those that are working in home studios.'

RePro's View (cont)

Key issues

'Income is always a prime concern. We are currently working to acquire performance income through various routes. We are also always concerned with technology and how that is developing. We are the people who are at the sharp end of the new recording technologies. The way that technology is moving so quickly means that very often problems are foisted on the recording producer which should not be his problems at all. As far as the profession is concerned, we are becoming more and more involved in all kinds of areas throughout the industry because we believe that the producer is the most pivotal person in the whole process of making the products that make this industry survive. We have a very important role to play in the way the industry develops in this extraordinary transitional period during the digitisation of the industry. The implications for revenue streams when sales are made by transmission are profound, and the way that the entire industry is financed may change. We want to make sure producers will be involved in this change and properly compensated for the increasing role they will be playing.'

9 The knowledge

A s I said earlier, you can't become a record producer without having a deep understanding of your chosen style of music. It has to be up to you to gain this understanding and to invent ways in which you can extend the boundaries of this style, perhaps further than anyone could have imagined. You will however also need a knowledge of the mechanics of record production, and skills in using the resources at your disposal to best advantage. With these matters I can help, at least enough to put you on the right track.

In this chapter, I am going to list many of the technical details you need to know to become a record producer, but it's up to you to do the leg work and actually acquire the knowledge. Just as a would-be taxi driver is issued with an A to Z map but has to go out and drive the streets until all the possible routes have become second nature. Let's start with …

Music

Record producers don't need to know anything about written music. There are plenty of people who would probably tell you otherwise, but they are probably classically trained musicians who are merely dabbling in the real business of music and not actual record producers themselves. As a classically trained musician, I realised a long time ago that the dots are only a means to an end, but so many so-called musicians really do believe that a musical score actually is music.

Can't read music? No problem!
Music of course doesn't exist until it is played, or a recording of that music is played. A printed sheet can only ever be a rough guide to what the music is supposed to sound like. If you do read music, beware that it is all too easy to get bogged down in the notes and not really listen to the music – you can't see the wood for the trees, to quote an old saying with a similar meaning.

Having said this, some of the terminology of music notation is commonly used among non-reading musicians. If one member of a band said, 'I think we should throw in a 5/4 bar and change the hihat to a triplet rhythm', and you didn't understand what he was on about then you might feel inclined to worry just a little. Don't

If you don't read music, don't ever let yourself think that you are at a disadvantage – quite the reverse in fact since you are totally free to listen and create. You can always hire an arranger as and when you need to.

waste your time on worrying about what you don't know yet – just ask them to try it, and if it sounds good to you then store that phrase in your memory for future reference!

I would say that you are much better off picking up this type of knowledge as and when you need it and be driven by the needs of the music, rather than having your head stuffed full of the technicalities on which formal tuition tends to concentrate. The main thing is to be around musicians and learn the vocabulary of your chosen style of music. And if you don't know the proper term for the idea you want to communicate to a musician – just sing it! That will get the message across in a much more direct way.

If you are working with samplers and sequencers, then you will need to understand the letter names of musical notes and also time signatures. Unfortunately, no-one has yet invented a computer that you can sing to and say you want it to sound like this! So, as well as having to be technically knowledgeable about the equipment, you have to know a lot of musical technicalities too – or work with a programmer who knows it all.

Just imagine ...

Beside the notes and rhythms of music, there is another aspect which is much more difficult to master – the sound of music. It's difficult enough to imagine notes in your head, and you can always play them on a keyboard or guitar if need be, but if you are going to be a truly creative producer then you will have to be able to 'hear' the sounds of different combinations of instruments before even a note has been played (and before the session musicians have been booked!). What's more, you are going to have to be able to apply this to all the sonic manipulation and trickery the recording studio has to offer.

Trial and error, and sometimes sheer luck, play an important part in studio recording, but they will only get you so far. The best producers can do a lot of the creative work in their imagination, and then set about making it happen for real on tape.

Use your lugs

To develop your musical imagination you should start with whatever knowledge of music and recording you have already, then listen to a favourite CD and try to work out exactly how every sound was created. At first you will say, 'Ah yes, that's a bass guitar', and you will probably think that is all there is to it. An experienced producer on the other hand will probably hear much deeper into the sound and say that it's a Fender Precision bass with flat wound strings, played with a plectrum into a valve amplifier, miked with a dynamic mic at a distance of a couple of metres and mixed with the DI (direct inject) feed into the console. Really!

Similarly, you may hear a scratchy vocal effect set deep in the mix recurring every verse, while the producer will be able to say exactly which James Brown record it was sampled from, and probably make a pretty good guess at how much it cost to get copyright clearance! In fact, the more producing you do, the more detail you will hear in your records.

To give an example, I have recently been exploring what variations in sound I can get with reverb on low frequency instruments such as bass drum, bass guitar and bass synth. And now that my ears are tuned into this sound I am amazed at how much low frequency reverb I can hear on CDs in my collection that I never even noticed was there before. The more deeply you can listen into recordings, the more you will develop your musical imagination.

Instruments

As I have previously mentioned, you don't have to be able to play an instrument or program a computer to be a producer as long as you can get hold of people who can do these things for you. If fact, you are probably much better off just sitting back and listening rather than getting too involved with the nuts and bolts. But you do have to know what sounds are available from all the different instruments in common – and not so common – use.

Pop music instruments

Staples in the popular music world of course include acoustic and electric guitars, bass guitar, keyboards, drums, samplers and turntables. But you need to know about the subtleties on offer within each group of instruments.

Even a non-guitarist knows that there are electric and acoustic guitars, for example, but a producer should have a mental list of all the different types available, and mental sonic images of the sounds they produce:

- Nylon strung acoustic (classical guitar)
- Steel strung acoustic
- 12 string acoustic
- Electric (non-humbucking pickups)
- Electric (humbucking pickups)

- 12 string electric
- Electro-acoustic
- Bass guitar (electric and acoustic)
- Mandolin and mandola
- Banjo
- Resonator (Dobro)
- Pedal steel and Hawaiian

So you wouldn't just be thinking, 'Let's try a guitar on this track', you would be consulting your mental database of sounds, and almost certainly subdividing this list further. For example, among electro-acoustic guitars, an Ovation has a very different sound to a Takamine or Washburn. Among electric guitars, the Fender Stratocaster and Gibson Les Paul (to name two classic models) are quite unlike each other sonically. The way the instrument is played makes a big difference too. Plectrum and fingerpicking styles are obviously different techniques – but even the thickness of a plectrum can change the guitar's sound enormously.

Orchestral instruments

With orchestral instruments, there is a vast range of sounds on offer and the way you will get to understand what they can do, individually and in combination, is by listening to CDs, or by getting hold of a CD-ROM about musical instruments which will give you at least an introduction to what they sound like.

As I said earlier about the way a producer listens to a recording, there is very much more to any instrument, or any group of instruments, than would be immediately obvious to anyone listening to them seriously for the first time. And however much you feel you understand an instrument already, there is always more that can be learned, as any good player will tell you.

Synths and samplers

In the case of electronic keyboard instruments, the strange thing is that it is easy to be overwhelmed by the vast number of seemingly different sounds a synth can produce, and it is tempting to think that keyboards are all you would ever need to make a record. This is not the case however, since even the latest synths produce sounds that are insufficiently complex to satisfy the human ear for long, and it is very difficult to make an all-synth album and make it good enough to listen to over and over.

The same applies to samplers, and as a producer you will find yourself working very much harder to get an interesting sound than if you had used conventional instruments. Note that I'm not saying that you shouldn't use synths and samplers, just don't fall into the trap of thinking that they are going to make your life easier. In reality, you are going to have to put your creativity into overdrive.

Equipment

Some studios have so much equipment that you might think it is impossible for one person to understand it all. Unless you have an aptitude for equipment, and you want to become a producer through the engineering route, I suggest you keep your hands off and leave it to the engineer! You should know what everything does however. I will leave any gaps in your existing knowledge to your own research, but you need to know about the following, and understand what implications they have on the sound of the recording:

- Microphones
- Mixing console
- Multitrack recorder (analogue and digital)
- Stereo recorder
- Loudspeakers (often called monitors)
- Compressor
- Noise gate
- Digital reverb unit
- Pitch changer
- Multi-effects unit

Effects

There are two types of effects: those which come in a rack mounting unit or as a guitarist's stomp box, and those which are painstakingly created with the imaginative use of studio technology. 'Instant' effects are often part and parcel of a musician's sound, particularly in the case of guitarists, and include wah-wah, phaser, flanger, chorus, delay and distortion. You will of course need to get to know what all of these effects sound like so that you know when to use them. (Sometimes you'll have difficulty getting guitarists not to use them!).

Certain styles of music require the recording to be pretty much an accurate representation of what would actually be heard on stage. An 'honest' recording if you like, where effects are used sparingly merely to enhance what is already there. Most recordings use artificial reverberation, and you will need to explore the capabilities of pro studio favourites such as the Lexicon 224X and 480L digital reverb units thoroughly. But often you will need to go beyond the obvious to create a new sound world in the studio, and you may not be able to find what you want prepackaged into a handy unit.

To explain all the effects that are possible in the studio would require a whole shelf of books, not just part of one chapter, and you can only really learn from real life experience in the studio. Remember that as a producer, you don't necessarily have to know how to create each effect, you only have to know what they sound like and have an imagination for what you could do with them. So each time you work with recording equipment or in a studio, try to find out a little more about EQ, reverb, compression, gating, delay, pitch changing and all the other effects. Learn by listening so that next time you need to thicken up a limp lead vocal, you know that it should be EQed, compressed and given some delay and reverb. And if it's really weak you'll know that adding a slightly pitched changed version to the original will bolster it up, at the expense of making it sound just a little less human.

> If it all sounds complex and difficult, that's because it is. But you don't have to know all about studio technicalities straight away, as long as you have good people working with you and you know what you want to achieve musically.

How to become …

Since you are almost at the end of the book, I suppose I should actually tell you how to become a record producer since you have been waiting so long! For your benefit I have distilled the information I have obtained from top producers into a few simple guidelines:

- If you want to learn how to produce, just get in a studio and do it. You can learn a lot from books, quality home and project studio recording magazines such as *Sound on Sound* and recording courses, but you can only really learn how to produce by working in a commercial studio.
- To become a producer through the engineering route, get into a good recording studio by writing lots of letters to every studio you hear of. When you have written to them all with no success, wait three months and write again. You may have to write hundreds of letters to get one interview.
- To become a producer through the musician route, get in with a band or other musicians who are regularly recording in good studios. Observe everything and learn.

- Approach a band and offer them studio time at your expense, with an agreement to share in any profits of course. When you take the recordings to a record company, make sure the A&R manager knows that you are the producer and it is you that has made the band sound great. Liaise with the band's management and try to get them to share in recording costs.
- Find a singer and arrange and produce the instrumental backing, preferably in a professional studio. Take the tapes to a record company, or use them to get professional management for the artist. Record companies prefer acts who already have management.
- Make a recording and release it yourself on your own label. If it sells a couple of thousand or more, it's enough to make a record company take you seriously.
- Once again, just do it!

So that's it. How to become a record producer is no big secret. If you have talent and determination you can start to become one today by saving some money towards your first session in a pro studio with a pro engineer. At this very first session, you will indeed be a producer and you will be doing exactly the work that a successful record producer does.

How far you get in the business is up to you – only a very few can carve out a successful, continuing career. But when you do achieve recognised producer status, make sure you write to me via the publisher of this book. You don't have to thank me because I haven't done anything except to point you in the right direction. Send me a copy of the record or CD and I will have the satisfaction that I played a very, very small part in its creation. You will have the satisfaction of achieving something that is the ambition of everyone, probably hundreds of thousands of people the world over, with an interest in recording music. You will have become a Record Producer!

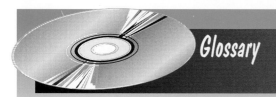

A&R
The Artists and Repertoire (or Artists and Recording) department of a record company. The A&R manager selects acts and oversees the recording process.

ADAT
Eight track digital multitrack recorder. Multiple units can easily be synchronised together.

Analogue
Method of handling sound signals as electrical voltages or magnetism. Analogue tape recorders are popular for their distinctive sound.

APRS
Association of Professional Recording Services. The industry organisation representing recording studios in the UK.

Assistant engineer
A trainee recording engineer who assists the engineer by setting up microphones and other basic tasks.

Backing track
The basic instrumentation of a song to which vocals and overdubs will be added.

Bouncing
Mixing two or more tracks on the multitrack tape onto one, or three or more tracks onto two in stereo, to free tracks for further use.

Click track
A metronomic click, usually provided by a drum machine, recorded on one track of the multitrack as a timing reference. Makes it easier to edit the multitrack.

Compiling (comping)
Making one good track out of several takes. Commonly done with vocals.

Compressor
A device to reduce the difference between loud and quiet sounds. Used correctly can make vocals stronger.

DAT
Digital Audio Tape. The most common stereo mastering format.

Digital
Method of handling sound signals as sequences of numbers. Has the advantage of low noise and low distortion. Digital disk recording systems offer instantaneous fast wind and rewind and flexibility of editing.

Distortion
Used as a creative effect by guitarists. Elsewhere in the recording studio distortion can result from faulty equipment or by the engineer setting levels too high.

Drop in
See 'Punch in'.

Drum machine
An electronic drummer that always plays in time and never gets drunk.

DTRS
Eight track digital multitrack recording system. Multiple units can easily be synchronised together.

Editing
Selecting parts of a recording, or of several takes of a recording and combining them together.

Effects
Devices or techniques to make a sound more interesting. Includes chorus, compression, delay, distortion, flanging, gating, phasing, pitch changing and reverb.

EQ (equaliser)
Alters the frequency balance of a sound.

Engineer
The recording engineer will operate the equipment in the studio and help the producer obtain the sound he or she wants. The engineer will also perform the mix, under the producer's supervision.

Fixer
See 'Session agent'.

Gate
See 'Noise gate'.

Guide track
Usually a guide vocal recorded with the backing tracks with the intention of later replacement.

Hard disk
Recording system using hard disks or optical disks similar to those used in computers. Compared to tape, hard disk systems offer great flexibility of editing.

Hire company
A company that hires out recording and/or musical equipment to producers. The record company usually picks up the bill.

Leslie
A loudspeaker cabinet with rotating drive units. Commonly used with organs.

Loudspeakers
See 'Monitors'.

Mastering
The process of transferring the stereo master recording to CD. At this stage, EQ, compression and crossfades can be applied.

MCPS
Mechanical Copyright Protection Society. The body administering the right of composers and music publishers to allow sound recordings of their works, or copies of these recordings, to be made.

Microphone
Converts sound to an electrical signal.

MIDI
Modern synthesisers, samplers and sequencers (which usually run on a personal computer) conform to the MIDI (Musical Instrument Digital Interface) standard which means that they can be linked and operated together.

Mixing
The process of converting the eight to forty-eight tracks of a multitrack recording to stereo.

Mixing console
The control centre of the studio through which all signals pass during recording and mixing.

Monitors
Recording studios have large high quality monitors which provide an accurate reference to the recorded sound quality.

Multitrack recorder
A tape (analogue or digital) or hard disk recorder with between eight and forty-eight separate tracks.

Near field monitors
Small monitors which approximate the sound of a typical hifi system.

Noise gate
A device for cutting out background noise during pauses when an instrument is not playing. Can also be used for creative effects.

Orchestral contractor
A session agent or fixer specialising in orchestral instruments.

Overdub
A track recorded onto a multitrack tape after the backing tracks.

Punch in
Technique used to repair a short faulty passage in an otherwise good instrumental or vocal recording.

RePro
The Guild of Recording Producers, Directors and Engineers.

Reverb
A type of effect. Digital reverberation units are used to simulate the natural reverberation of a room or space.

Sampler
A device used to imitate the sound of conventional instruments using actual digital recordings of the instrument. Also used to sample sections of existing recordings for use in new productions. Can also be used to facilitate the recording process.

Sequencer
A device used to record the keys pressed on a MIDI keyboard rather than an audio signal. Used with samplers and synthesisers, a sequencer can complement or replace a multitrack recorder.

Session agent
An employment agency supplying musicians and vocalists for recording sessions.

Session musician
A freelance musician who specialises in recording.

Stereo recorder
An analogue or digital recorder upon which the finished stereo mix is made.

Synchroniser
A device used to synchronise a MIDI sequencer with a multitrack recorder, or to synchronise two multitrack recorders, or a multitrack recorder to a video.

Take
An attempt at making a recording.

Tape op
See 'Assistant engineer'

Tube
See 'Valve'.

Valve
Amplifiers that use valves as their active devices are popular for their slightly distorted, 'warm' sound quality.

Professional associations

APC (Association of Professional Composers), The Penthouse, 4 Brook Street, London W1Y 1AA, Tel 0171 629 0992

APRS (Association of Professional Recording Services), 2 Windsor Square, Silver Street, Reading, Berks RG1 2TH, Tel 01734 756218

ASCAP, Suite 10/11, 52 Haymarket, London SW11 4RP, Tel 0171 973 0069

Audio Engineering Society, P O Box 645, Slough, Bucks SL1 8BJ, Tel 01628 663725

BASCA (British Association of Songwriters Composers & Authors), The Penthouse, 4, Brook Street, London W1Y 1AA, Tel 0171 629 0992

BPI (British Phonographic Institute), 25 Saville Row, London W1X 1AA, Tel 0171 287 4422

British Music Industry, 79 Harley House, Marylebone Road, London NW1 5HN, Tel 0171 935 8517

MCPS (Mechanical Copyright Protection Society), Edgar House, 41 Streatham High Road, London SW16 1ER, Tel 0181 769 4400

Music Industries Association, 7 The Avenue, Datchet, Slough, Berks SL3 9DH, Tel 01753 541 963,

Music Publishers Association, 3rd Floor, Strandgate, 18/20 York Buildings, London WC2N 6JU, Tel 0171 839 7779

Musicians Union, 60-62 Clapham Road, London SW9 0JJ, Tel 0171 582 5566

Sound & Communication Industries Federation, 4-8 High Street Burnham, Slough SL1 7JH, Tel 01628 667 633

P@MRA (Performing Artists' Media Rights Society), 80 Borough High Street, London SE1 1LL, Tel 0171 378 6777

Performing Right Society, 29-33 Berners Street, London W1P 4AA, Tel 0171 580 5544

PPL (Phonographic Performance Ltd), Ganton House, 14-22 Ganton Street, London W1V 1LB, Tel 0171 437 0311

RePro, (The Guild of Recording Producers, Directors and Engineers), 68 Cleveland Street, London SW13 0AH, Tel 0181 876 3411,

VPL (Video Performance Ltd), Ganton House, 14-22 Ganton Street, London W1V 1LB, Tel 0171 437 0311, Fax 0171 734 2966

College courses

There are many college courses concerned with music and recording, so make sure you get onto the course that is right for you. Few colleges offer specialised recording production courses, although courses suitable for musicians, programmers and engineers are widely available. If you are interested in recording, make sure you get onto a recording course and not one that is more appropriate for live sound engineers. Judge a course by the experience in the music and recording industry of the teaching staff, and the amount of hands-on time you get with the equipment. Ask about class sizes in practical sessions. Often a college that has a number of small-scale studio setups will offer more value than a college that has a single showpiece studio that few students ever get to work in. Remember that no college can give you the magic key that will unlock the door to success. As your course progresses you must also find other opportunities to work with musicians and make recordings in the real world. The certificate you will earn on your course may be nice to look at, but you will only be a record producer when you receive your first fee or royalty cheque!

Able Studio, 87 Wesley Road, South Harrow, Middlesex HA2 8HB,
Alchemea, 2-18 Brittania Row, The Angel London N1 8QH, Tel 0171 359 4035
Anglia Polytechnic University, East Road, Cambridge, Cambs CB1 1PT, Tel 01223 63271
Arnold & Carlton College, Digby Avenue, Nottingham NG6 3DR, Tel 0115 952 0052
Barnsley College, Church Street, Barnsley, S.Yorks S70 2AX, Tel 01226 73
Barton Peveril College, Cedar Road, Eastleigh, Hants SO50 5ZA, Tel 01703 367200
Bournemouth University, Music Department, Talbot Campus, Fern Barrow, Poole, Dorset BH12 5BB, Tel 01202 524111
Bournemouth & Poole College of Further Education, North Road, Parkstone, Poole, Dorset BH14 OLS, Tel 01202 205902
Bradford & Ilkley Comm College, Great Horton Road, Bradford, W. Yorks BD7 1AY, Tel 01274753313
Bretton Hall, Music Dept., West Bretton, `Wakefield, W.Yorks WF4 4LG, Tel 01924 830261
Bridgewater College, Bath Road, Bridgewater, Somerset TA6 4PZ, Tel 01823 333451
Bristol University, Music Dept. Senate House, Tyndall Avenue, Bristol, Avon BS8 1TH, Tel 01179 303030
Central School of Speech & Drama, Embassy Theatre, 64 Eaton Avenue, London NW3 3HY, Tel 0171 722 8183
Charles Keene College, Sector of Technology, Painter Street, Leicester LE1 3WA, Tel 0116 2516037
Chichester College of Technology, Dept of Music & Drama, Chitec Studio, Chichester, Sussex PO19 1SB, Tel 01241 786321
Christ Church College, Music Dept. North Holmes Road, Canterbury, Kent CT1 1QU, Tel 01227 782420
City College Manchester, Barlow Moor Road, West Didsbury, Greater Manchester M20 8PQ, Tel 0161 434 4821
City of Leeds College of Music, Dept of Musical Instrument Technology, Cookridge Street, Leeds, W. Yorks LS2 8BH Tel 01132 452069
City of Liverpool Community College, Mabel Fletcher Centre, Waver street, Liverpool L15 4JB,
City of London Polytechnic, 41-71 Commercial Road, London E1 1LA, Tel 0171 320 1000

City University, The Music Department, Northampton Square, London EC1V OHB

City of Westminster College, Paddington Green, London W2 1NB, Tel 0171 723 8826

Clarendon College Performing Arts, Pelham Street, Nottingham

Coventry Centre for the Performing Arts, Leasowes Avenue, Coventry CV3 6BH, Tel 01203 418868

Colchester Institute, Sheepden Road, Colchester, Essex CO3 3LL, Tel 01206 718000, Tel 01206 763041

Crawley College, College Road, Crawley, W.Sussex BH10 1NR,

Earth Studios, 163 Gerrard Street, Lozells, Birmingham, W.MIDS B19 2AP, Tel 0121 554 7424

East Birmingham College, Garretts Green Lane, Birmingham, W.Mids B33 OTS, Tel 0121 743 4471

Essex Music Centre, West Mead, Sible Hedingham, Essex CO9 1PU, Tel 01787 461902

Estover Community College, Miller Way, Estover, Plymouth PL6 8UN, Tel 01752 781714 Tel 01752 788569, 100764.3151@compuserve.com

Falkirk College of Technology, Tel 01324 624981 Tel 01324 632 86

Farnborough College of Technology, Boundary Road, Farnborough, Hants GU14 6SB

Goldsmith College, University of London, Lewisham Way, New Cross, London SE14 6NW, Tel 0181 692 7171

Featherstone High School, 11 Montague Way, Southall, EALING, London

Gateway School of Music, Kingston Hill Centre, Kingston Hill, Surrey KT2 7LB

Harlow College, College Square, The High, Harlow, Essex CM20 1LT, Tel 01279 441288

Hinckley College, London Road, Hinckley, Leicestershire LE10 1HQ Tel 01455 251222

Huddersfield Technical College, Dept of Musical Instrument Technology, New North Road, Huddersfield, Yorkshire HD1 5NN, Tel 01484 536521

Hull College of FE, Dept of Music, Queens Gardens, Hull, Humberside

Islington Music Workshop, 44 Peartree Street, London EC1V 3SB, Tel 0171 608 0231

Jewel & Esk Valley College, Milton Road Centre, 24 Milton Road East Edinburgh EH15 2PP, Tel 0131 669 8461

Kidderminster College, Hoo Road, Kidderminster, Worcestershire DY10 1LX, Tel 01562 820811

Kingston University, Dept of Music, Penhryn Road, Kingston upon Thames, Surrey, KT1 2EE Tel 0181 547 2000

Lambeth College, Norwood Centre, Knights Hill, London SE27 0TX

Leeds Metropolitan University, Calverley Street, Leeds, W Yorks LS1 3HE, Tel 01132 832600

London Guildhall University, 117-119 Houndsditch, London EC3A 7BU, Tel 0171 320 1000

Manchester School of Sound Recording, 10 Tariff Street, Manchester M1 2FF, Tel 0161 228 1830

Media Production Facilities, Bon Marche Building, Ferndale Road, Brixton, London, SW9 8EJ, Tel 0171 737 7152

Napier University, Dept of Photo Film & TV, 6/7 Coats Place, Edinburgh, Scotland EH3 7AA, Tel 0131 455 2614

National Institute of Recording Arts, Elsinore Road, Old Trafford, Manchester M16 OWG

Neath College, Dry-y-Felin Road, Neath Wales SA 10 7RF, Tel 01639 634271

Newark & Sherwood College, Friary Road, Newark, Notts NG 24 1BP, Tel 01636 705 921

Newark Technical College, Dept of Musical Instrument Technology, Chauntry Park, Newark, Notts NG24 1BP, Tel 01636 705921

Newcastle College, School of Music, Maple Terrace, Newcastle upon Tyne, NE4 7SA, Tel 0191 273 8866

Newcastle College, John Marley Centre, Muscott Groveoff, Wicham View, Newcastle upon Tyne, NE15 6TT

Newcastle College, Rye Hill Campus, Scotswood Road, Newcastle upon Tyne NE4 7SA Tel 0191 233 8866

Newham College of Further Education, Stratford Campus, Welfare Road, London E15 4HT, Tel 0181 257 4000

North Cheshire College, Cheshire Music Studio, Padgate Campus, Warrington, Cheshire WA2 0DB,

North Glasgow College, Springburn Campus, 110 Flemington Street, Glasgow, Scotland G21 4BX, Tel 0141 558 90

Oldham College, Dept of Performing Arts, Rochdale Road, Oldham, Lancs OL9 6AA, Tel 0161 624 5214

Parkland Studios, The Spinney, Forest Road, Denmead, Waterlooville, Hants PO7 6TZ, Tel 01705 258985

Perth College of FE, Crieff Road, Perth, Scotland, PH1 2NX Tel 01738 21171

Polytechnic of N London, Dept of Elec & Comm Engng, Holloway Road, London N7 8DB, Tel 0171 607 2789

Preston College, The Park School, Moor Park Avenue, Preston, Lancs PR1 6AP, Tel 01772 254145

Richard Huish College, South Road, Taunton, Devon TA1 3DZ

Right Track Studios, Woodbine House, Marden, Hereford HR1 3DX, Tel 01432 880442

Rose Bruford College, Lamorbey Park, Sidcup, Kent DA15 9DF, Tel 0181 300 3024

Royal College of Music, Prince Consort Road, London SW7 2BS, Tel 0171 589 3643

Salford University College, Frederick Road, Salford, Manchester M6 6PU, Tel 0161 636 6541

School Of Audio Engineering, United House, North Road, London N7, Tel 0171 609 2653

School of Cultural Studies, Sheffield Hallam University, Psalter Lane, Sheffield, Yorkshire S11 8UZ, Tel 01142 532607

Selhurst College, The Crescent, Croydon, Surrey CRO 2LY,

South Thames College, Wandsworth High Street, London SW18 2PP, Tel 0181 870 2241 X 325 Tel 0181 874 6163

St Loyes College, Topsham Road, Exeter, Devon EX2 6EP, Tel 01392 55428,

Stow College, 43 Shamrock Street, Glasgow, Scotland G4 9LD, Tel 0141 332 1786

Sandown College, Dept of Musical Instrument Technology, Sandown Road, Liverpool L15 4JB, Tel 0151 733 5511

Sandwell College of FHE, The Media Group, Wednesbury Campus, Woden Rd South Wednesbury, W.Mids WS10 OPE, Tel 0121 556 6000

South Downs College, Adult Education Centre, College Road, Havant, Hants PO7 8AA, Tel 01705 376700

South Manchester College, Abraham Moss Centre, Crescent Road, Manchester M8 6UF, Tel 0161 740 9438

The Music Room, 1st Floor, Alford House, Alford Place, Aberdeen AB10 1YB, Tel 01224 580058

The Stables, Wavendon, Milton Keynes, Buckinghamshiree MK17 8LT, Tel 01908 670306

Thames Valley University, London College of Music, St Mary's Road, Ealing, London W5 5RF, Tel 0181 231 2364

Thames Valley University, School of TIS, Wellington Street, Slough, SL1 1YB

Ulster University, Dept of Music, Cromore Road, Coleraine, Londonderry BT32 1SA, Tel 01265 44141

University of Birmingham, Department of Music, Edgbaston, Birmingham, W. Mids B515 2TT, Tel 0121 414 3344

University of Brighton, Cockroft Building, Moulscoomb, Brighton, Sussex BN2 4GJ

University College, Salford, Dept of Performing Arts & Media Studies, Adelphi Campus, Peru Street, Salford, Manchester M3 6EQ, Tel 0161 834 6633

University of Derby, Kedleston Road, Derby, Derbyshire DE22 1GB, Tel 01332 622222

University of East Anglia, Norwich, Norfolk NR4 7TJ, Tel 01603 56161

University of Hertfordshire, College Lane, Hatfield, Herts AL10 9AB, Tel 01707 279000

University of Keele, Dept of Music, Keele, Staffordshire ST5 5BG, Tel 01782 621111

University of Liverpool, Institute of Popular Music, PO Box 147, Liverpool L69 3BX, Tel 0151 794 31

University of Newcastle upon Tyne, Dept of Music, Armstrong Building, Newcastle upon Tyne, NE1 7RU Tel 0191 222 6000

University of North London, 166-220 Holloway Road, London N7 8DB, Tel 0171 607 2789

University of Nottingham, Music Dept, University Park, Nottingham, Notts NG7 4RD,

University of Reading, Whiteknights, PO Box 217, Reading, Berks RG6 2AH, Tel 01734 875123

University of Surrey, Dept of Music, Guildford, Surrey GU2 5XH, Tel 01483 571281

University of Sussex, Brighton Rock Arts, Falmer, Brighton, Sussex BN1 9ON, Tel 01273 678

University of Wales, Dept of Music, Aberystwyth, King Street, Aberystwyth, Dyfed, Tel 01970 623111

University of Wales, Dept of Music, Bangor, College Road, Bangor Wales LL57 2DG, Tel 01248 382190

University of Westminster, Harrow School of Design & Media, Warford Road, Northwick Park, Harrow HA1 3TP, Tel 0171 911 5000

University of York, Dept of Music, Heslington, York YO1 5DD, Tel 01904 433535

Upbury Manor School, Marlborough Road, Gillingham, KENT ME7 5AT

Walsall College of Art, Dept of Music, Walsall, W. Mids, Tel 01924 3705

Wakefield Disrict College, Margaret Street, Wakefield, Yorks WS1 2DH, Tel 01924 3705

Warrington Collegiate Institute, Padgate Campus, Fearnhead Lane, Warrington, Cheshire WA2 ODB

West Cumbria College, Flatt Walls, Whitehaven, Cumbria CA28 7RN,

West Kent College, Brook Street, Tonbridge, Kent TN9 2PW, Tel 01732 358101

Index